# ROUTLEDGE LIBRARY EDITIONS: CHRISTIANITY

Volume 10

# THE CHRISTIAN MYSTERY

# THE CHRISTIAN MYSTERY
An Exposition of Esoteric Christianity

LOIS LANG-SIMS

LONDON AND NEW YORK

This edition first published in 2021
by Routledge
2 Park Square, Milton Park, Abingdon, Oxon OX14 4RN

and by Routledge
52 Vanderbilt Avenue, New York, NY 10017

*Routledge is an imprint of the Taylor & Francis Group, an informa business*

First published 1980 Allen & Unwin. Copyright 1980 George Allen & Unwin Ltd.

All rights reserved. No part of this book may be reprinted or reproduced or utilised in any form or by any electronic, mechanical, or other means, now known or hereafter invented, including photocopying and recording, or in any information storage or retrieval system, without permission in writing from the publishers.

*Trademark notice*: Product or corporate names may be trademarks or registered trademarks, and are used only for identification and explanation without intent to infringe.

*British Library Cataloguing in Publication Data*
A catalogue record for this book is available from the British Library

ISBN: 978-0-367-62307-4 (Set)
ISBN: 978-1-003-10879-5 (Set) (ebk)
ISBN: 978-0-367-62510-8 (Volume 10) (hbk)
ISBN: 978-0-367-63152-9 (Volume 10) (pbk)
ISBN: 978-1-003-10948-8 (Volume 10) (ebk)

**Publisher's Note**
The publisher has gone to great lengths to ensure the quality of this reprint but points out that some imperfections in the original copies may be apparent.

**Disclaimer**
The publisher has made every effort to trace copyright holders and would welcome correspondence from those they have been unable to trace.

# The Christian Mystery

## An Exposition of Esoteric Christianity

*By*
LOIS LANG-SIMS

London
GEORGE ALLEN & UNWIN
Boston           Sydney

First published in 1980

This book is copyright under the Berne Convention. All rights are reserved. Apart from any fair dealing for the purpose of private study, research, criticism or review, as permitted under the Copyright Act, 1956, no part of this publication may be reproduced, stored in a retrieval system, or transmitted, in any form or by any means, electronic, electrical, chemical, mechanical, optical, photocopying, recording or otherwise, without the prior permission of the copyright owner. Enquiries should be sent to the publishers at the undermentioned address:

GEORGE ALLEN & UNWIN LTD
40 Museum Street, London WC1A 1LU

© George Allen & Unwin (Publishers) Ltd, 1980

---

**British Library Cataloguing in Publication Data**

Lane-Sims, Lois
   The Christian mystery.
   1. Theology, Doctrinal
   I. Title
   230   BT77.3   80-41004

ISBN 0-04-200038-6

---

Set in 11 on 12 point Ehrhardt by Servis Filmsetting Ltd, Manchester
and printed in Great Britain
by Biddles Ltd, Guildford, Surrey

# Contents

| | | |
|---|---|---|
| 1 | The Reality of the Myth | page 1 |
| 2 | The Heart of the Mystery | 9 |
| 3 | In the Beginning | 14 |
| 4 | The Adam | 19 |
| 5 | The Mystery of Sin | 26 |
| 6 | The Word Made Flesh | 33 |
| 7 | The Mystery of the Virgin | 40 |
| 8 | The Mystery of St John | 46 |
| 9 | The Mysteries of the Infant Christ | 51 |
| 10 | The Ministry of Jesus | 59 |
| 11 | The Vigil of the Passion | 68 |
| 12 | The Cross | 79 |
| 13 | The Risen Body | 91 |
| 14 | The Ascent of the Son and the Descent of the Spirit | 100 |
| 15 | Our Lady in Heaven | 108 |
| 16 | The Last Things | 113 |
| 17 | The World as Sacrament | 121 |
| 18 | Time as Sacrament | 128 |
| 19 | Man as Sacrament | 137 |
| 20 | God as Sacrament | 144 |

Extract from *The Dream of the Rood* is from *Earliest English Poems* trans. Michael Alexander (Penguin Books).
Extract from *Hymn of the Soul* is from the trans. by A. A. Bevan in *Texts & Studies* 1897.
All quotations from St. John of the Cross are from the translation by Roy Campbell (Harvill/Collins).
All quotations from Julian of Norwich are from the translation by James Walsh. (A. Clarke Books).
Quotations from Rumi from the translation by R. A. Nicholson (George Allen & Unwin).
Poem by Joost van der Vondel is quoted in *Sacred & Profane Beauty* by Gerardus Van der Leeuw trans. David Green (Weidenfeld & Nicholson).

*To Marco*

# Chapter One

# *The Reality of the Myth*

It has been said – and this indeed is the essence of all the great religious traditions of the world: *know thyself*.

It has also been said that no man is an island. No one of us can, by turning inwards, discover the truth about himself, as an individual person and in his innermost being *as man*, unless he is at the same time in a state of communion – with others, and with nature, and (but all else is included in this, and without it no other and lesser form of communion can exist), with God. As an aspect of this being-in-communion, we are nourished on all the interpenetrating levels of our humanity, body, mind and spirit, by the Wisdom enshrined in tradition and continuously augmented in experience.

Until recently it was taken for granted that every man and woman was born into a particular religious tradition, that of his or her own people, and lived and died within it. Nowadays we are learning to ask ourselves: Who are my people? And the answer, as we are at last beginning to understand, can only be that 'my people' are all men everywhere who seek the face of God (that is to say, by definition, all those who are truly *human*, no matter what outward professions of 'belief' or 'disbelief' they may choose to make, or what words they may use or not use to describe the object of their search). However, we should not be misled by this new insight into supposing that we are now in a position to make a synthesis from all the traditions, appropriating what we choose and rejecting the rest. *A religious tradition is a unified whole*. Essentially it consists of the binding together of a complex mythology and the ritual activities which express that mythology, depending for their efficacy upon the setting aside of an area of 'sacred time' and 'sacred space', in a world which is thought of as being as yet incompletely 'sacred' or 'real'. By this means we are provided with a Wisdom and a Method for the progressive 'realisation' of our world as the dwelling-place of God.

Our own Myth is the story of the Christ.

But what do we mean when we speak of a 'Myth'?

From where we are we can look back down a straight line to the time of the parting of the ways (symbolised so beautifully in the Jewish and Christian traditions by the story of the sons of Noah who departed in three directions, implying that the fourth direction was a wasteland or, alternatively perhaps, the now forbidden garden).

> If all the seas were one sea
> What a *great* sea that would be!
> If all the trees were one tree,
> What a *great* Tree that would be!
> And if all the men were One Man
> What a *great* Man that would be!

The old rhyme expresses a truth we do not understand but know in our hearts. The One breaks up into the many. The many return to the One. These movements are primary and constitute the cause of our being, its eternal history and its end. Primitive man was aware of them as we are aware of them. 'Primitive' he may have been; but he was already *man*. He lifted up his heart to an everlasting source of light, and knew himself dimly as an infinitesimally tiny mirror of that light. He knew that he had come from God and was destined to return to Him. This realisation is marvellously expressed in a fragment which has come down to us from the ancient Mysteries associated with the name of Orpheus: 'I am the child of earth and starry heaven; but my race is of heaven alone.' So man acknowledges his divine origin; and, seeking the truth within himself, finds it only as he is able to transcend himself. Herein is a paradox; for this movement of transcendence may equally be understood as a turning within, a movement of penetration to the innermost core, where the apex and the centre meet in God Who is Immanence and Transcendence both. From this movement was derived what we may think of as the primary Myth.

## The Reality of the Myth

As a child awakens slowly to an understanding of the outside world, man awoke to an understanding of the reality which lies beyond and behind and within himself and his environment. He began to make images for the purpose of containing and preserving what he knew. He made a story about himself. Myth and ritual were born. Before long, as self-sufficient communities were formed, each one had its own Myth which represented for its members the three primary moments of time: the Beginning, the End, and the Movement between, which is but the summing up of a moment. This last was seen in terms of the peculiar vocation of the community bestowed upon it by God or the gods, expressed in its rites and realised in its work. Everyday actions were ritualised to conform to the Myth. Songs were sung and stories were told to develop its themes and pass them on from one generation to the next. Its earliest expression, perhaps, had been in music and miming dance; out of this sprang drama, which began as pure ritual and developed into ritual and play, an age-old combination which continuously through the ages has perpetuated myth. In this way there came into being innumerable systematised cults.

One of the richest and strangest of these cults was that which eventually took shape (and in doing so brought together the essential features of a variety of mythologies from earlier times which happened, just then, to be fermenting together in that particular corner of the earth) as a mystical interpretation of the life of Jesus who was called the Christ. The word comes from the Greek 'Christos' which means literally the Anointed One. It has acquired the meaning of 'the World Saviour', 'the Incarnate God'. Myth is revelation; and the Christian Myth is supremely the revelation of that great metaphysical paradox: the coinherence of earth in heaven and of heaven in earth. Myth is reality. The greater and the holier the Myth the more closely it approximates to what is truly 'happening' in the real world which lies behind our own. Even such a typical fairy-tale as that of the princess deposed by her maidservant and subjected to numerous ordeals before she is finally united to her prince, is closer to *what happens* in reality than the vast majority of episodes, including many of those we regard as tremendously important, which constitute the dream world of our day-to-day existence. *The Christ-story is supremely an account of what is happening*. Whether or not it happened in history – that is to say at some point along that particular line of historical time on which these words are being written and will eventually be read – is a question which need not, strictly speaking, be asked (although of course we do ask it) because the answer can in no way affect the validity of the story itself. *A Myth is a diagram of reality*. It is something quite other and infinitely more than an allegorical parable invented to illustrate some teaching or drive home some point. Plato's story of the shadows in the cave is a parable: his extraordinary vision of Creation in the *Timaeus* is a Myth, in the sense that he is actually translating metaphysical realities into images for the purpose of making himself understood and of *understanding himself*. Metaphysical realities can be known, *but in their own terms* they can never be expressed. They are *in themselves transcendent*. METAPHYSICAL TRUTHS CAN ONLY BE ADEQUATELY EXPRESSED IN TERMS OF MYTH.

The historical Jesus is not to be identified unreservedly with the mythical figure as this has been interpreted by the Church. The historical Jesus did not, as the Church has since done on His behalf, lay claim to being uniquely the once-and-for-all-time incarnation of the Godhead in man. The Gospels do not record that He said anything of Himself which cannot be said by everyman *in Christ*. That is to say He situated Himself at the metaphysical centre and spoke from there. Therefore, and considering the sublime holiness of His life and teachings and the mysterious manner of His death (if indeed it can be described as a 'death' in the ordinary sense), it is fitting that His Name and His mystical biography should stand for something more than, historically, He declared Himself to be. Provided we know what we are saying. Provided we understand that the Myth has appropriated Jesus. Before His time, and since, it existed, and exists, in the world in innumerable forms, as the story of a Divine Victim miraculously born, treacherously slain and triumphantly raised from the dead. Jesus, we are led to suppose, identified Himself with the role of the Divine Victim rather as an actor identifies himself with his allotted part. (The story would have been familiar to Him as part of the Mystery teachings of the sect of the Essenes with whom He studied in the desert as a prelude to His active work.) Many others have done the same. Basic to the teachings of the Mystery religions and the Schools which were either directly associated with them or at least permeated by influences of a similar kind was the mysterious idea of *role playing* in the sense of identifying oneself with some archetypal role conceived of as being played out in eternity – as some would say, 'by the gods'. (The Christian tradition does not speak of 'the gods'. This is because, within this tradition, the figures of Christ and His Mother comprehend them all.) The higher the initiation, the more complex and mysterious the identification was enabled to be.

The recorded sayings of Jesus are cryptic and ambiguous; and this is most obviously the case when He speaks of Himself. On the one hand it is clear that He was totally uninterested in professions of devotion addressed personally and emotionally to Him. (The emotional level is always personal; the level of mystical devotion is suprapersonal, suprapsychological, beyond the comprehension of anyone whose affections are fixed in the area of 'personal relationships'.) On the other hand, He repeatedly declares that in His Name, and in His Name only, His disciples shall be saved. 'I am the Way,' He tells them, in a moment of rapt exultation on the eve of His death, 'the Truth and the Life. No man cometh to the Father but by Me.' Lesser mystics have contented themselves with the negative self-definition: 'I am not: He *is*.' Jesus, going further, projects His identity into the innermost Heart of the Divine and speaks, if not always (and surely *not* always), at least in the supreme moments of His earthly existence, as the mouthpiece of That in which his personal individuality has been lost. So He has been misunderstood, inevitably but disastrously, by a Church which had, in any case, a vested interest in misunderstanding Him in this particular respect.

The claim of the historical Church (as distinct from the Mystical Church of the Myth, the meaning of which will be explained in due course) to be uniquely and exclusively the 'vessel of salvation' for the entire world, with the power to condemn an individual to damnation by depriving him of its sacraments, was based upon the prior claim that its founder was the one and only appearance upon earth of the One and Only God. The Church has misinterpreted its own Myth. The central figure of that Myth is greater than Jesus, greater than the Church, greater than Christianity, *greater than time*. The Christ-

## The Christian Mystery

Being is real upon a plane of reality that is infinitely more substantial than our own, possessing as it were a plenitude of reality which does not belong to the poor little world of clock time and three-dimensional space. (This is not to deny for a moment the glory and the beauty of this earth. Our 'world', when we understand it aright, is the point of intersection of innumerable interpenetrating worlds. The linear history which tends to dominate our thinking belongs to one of them, and that the most insignificant.) Therefore we must not, in speaking of the Christ-story as a myth, fall into the error of supposing that there is not *in reality* an Event corresponding to that Myth, a real Birth, a real Death, a real and for us unimaginably *substantial* Arising from the Dead. We tend to see things the wrong way round, as if the dream world in which we are accustomed to live must constitute our standard of what is real. But St Paul writes: 'Now we see through a glass darkly.' Now we only dream of what, in Eternity, is actually taking place.

*The Myth is a consistent whole*. When we begin to see how beautiful and almost flawless in its wholeness it actually is, we begin to understand it. This is the only way to understand it, because in appreciating its wholeness, we are enabled to see that anything which does not 'fit in' must somehow be wrong and the result of a misinterpretation or even, as must frequently have been the case, a deliberate distortion of the truth. The marvel is that, considering the appalling record of the Church in human cruelty and the machinations of power politics, the integrity of the Myth was preserved for so long. The concept of 'heresy', when properly understood, refers to the intentional spoliation of that integrity, the deliberate introduction of an element of incoherence. Heresy, real heresy, is (or was) a rarer thing than the Church has been prepared to admit. The Myth has developed as well by means of the so-called 'heresies' (which in most cases were not heresies at all but the restoration of a balance) as within the Councils of the orthodox. Most of the so-called 'heretics' were either rebels against some abuse, or mystics whose perspective had been altered by changes in their own levels of consciousness. Meister Eckhart and Boehme were victimised for nothing more heinous than the vast superiority of their spiritual knowledge over that of their persecutors; Dame Julian of Norwich intersperses her metaphysical revelations with

## The Reality of the Myth

pathetic protestations to the effect that 'in all things I believe as Holy Church preacheth and teacheth', while admitting again and again that she experienced the greatest difficulty in reconciling her 'shewings' (as she called them) with the kind of black-and-white logic typical of the theologians then as now; Simone Weil seems closer to the Cathars than to the official Church, which she steadfastly refused to join and by which, in an earlier age, she would almost certainly have been sent to her death. So the Mystery transcends the Church; and the Myth, which is the vehicle of the Mystery, is not, in its developed form, solely the creation even of baptised Christians. Simone Weil was not a baptised Christian; neither were the Cathars (or not in any sense that was recognised by the orthodox); neither most assuredly were those Sufi mystics of Islam, whose knowledge poured into the medieval Church, augmenting its own.

As we ponder the various aspects of the Mystery (represented by the Events of the Myth) it is essential to bear in mind that such matters as we are attempting to understand are not to be approached by a linear process of reasoning, point by point. Each separate doctrine of the Church is a *way into*, not one step in the direction of, the plenitude of the whole; so that if it were possible fully to comprehend a single doctrine or a single sacrament one would understand them all by means of that one. *The meaning expands from the centre*, as the Myth is unfolded from within, revealing itself a little more clearly in each successive unfolding. The great symbols move in and out of one another. This is not an easy concept to grasp; and we are grievously disadvantaged at the present time in that the two normal methods of imparting teachings such as these are unavailable to us. These two methods are: (1) in a slow process of initiation, by a qualified teacher, if possible in a circle of aspirants; and (2) as its native tongue is imparted to a child, by the total impact upon the individual of the tradition into which he is born and which surrounds him at every stage of his development. In the absence of these norms, we are bound to feel constantly perplexed. All that is intended in what follows is an indication of how we may begin to unravel the knots which are not in the teachings themselves but in our minds, the result of our present situation in the absence of a teacher who is qualified to teach. Here and now, we can only help each other to a limited extent. The seeker must seek for himself: in the liturgy of

*The Christian Mystery*

the Church, in the writings of the saints, in the architecture, paintings and music which the Christian tradition has produced – above all and all the time in his own heart, where the Myth is written and the symbols inscribed more clearly than in any book.

## Chapter Two

# *The Heart of the Mystery*

'Hail, O Cross,' cried St Andrew on the eve of his martyrdom, 'I know thy mystery, for the which thou art set up: for thou art planted in the world to establish the things that are unstable: and the one part of thee stretcheth up toward heaven that thou mayest signify the heavenly world: and another part of thee is spread out to the right hand and the left that it may put to flight the power of the evil one and gather into one the things that are scattered abroad. And another part of thee is planted in the earth, and securely set in the depth, that thou mayest join the things that are in the earth and under the earth unto the heavenly things. Well done, O Cross, that has bound down the mobility of the world! Well done, O shape of understanding that hast shaped the shapeless!'

The basic symbol of Christianity is the Rose Cross. This is the Cross with, superimposed upon it, the Mystic Rose. The Cross is contradiction, disintegration, the tearing apart of the Body of Christ. The Rose is consummation, resurrection, the flowering out of death of the principle of everlasting life. This principle can equally well be represented by a sunburst, or indeed (as in many early Roods and Crucifixes, before the intense concentration upon suffering which characterised medieval Catholicism produced representations of a grievously afflicted figure hanging limply from the Cross) by a Christ-in-glory, arms outstretched against the instrument of His triumph over death. In all these (and its many other) variations the 'Rose Cross' may be understood as a circle expanding and contracting upon a single point. Upon that central point rest the doctrines of the Christian faith, together with the seven sacraments.

The Myth of Christianity begins with the Creation, continues

## The Christian Mystery

with the Fall of the Angels, resulting in the Fall of Man, and goes on to relate how God the Father in His Infinite Mercy redeemed and forgave His Creation in the Person of Jesus, the Mystical Christ Who is Man in his union with God. Jesus, in the Myth, is something infinitely more than a single human being *in history* (that is to say along a single line of observed and recorded historical time) could possibly be. *The Myth is a concentration of time.* Whereas in the world as we know it there are countless millions of people, aeons of time, a seething complexity of events occurring in a chain-like continuum of cause and effect, in the Myth there are very few people and One is at the centre of them all. The events of the Myth are concentrated in the sense of being a compression of all that has ever happened and will ever happen into one comprehensible *story* which our minds can grasp and our understanding assimilate. We need to compress them still further, and see them as one single Event with an infinite number of aspects or modes whereby its essentiality may be tentatively approached. According to this way of seeing them, the episode of the Virgin Birth and that of the Recognition in the Garden (to take two instances picked entirely at random) are implicit each in each; they *are*, in a sense, each other, twin aspects of a single Movement, that of God towards man and man (in the person of Jesus) towards God. This Movement, this Event, takes place in Eternity or the Present. (In sequential or linear time there is, of course, no such thing as 'the present'.)

In the Middle Ages there was a delightful controversy in theological circles about the number of angels who were able to dance on the point of a needle all at once without falling off. This was a playful variation on the theme of the dimensionless point at the centre of the whorl of time, which being infinite is capable of supporting the entire angelic host. The point divides the future from the past. In terms of our earthly existence it is the moment of conception and the moment of death. In between these two moments our lives are a continuous process of expansion and contraction upon that point of eternity which is fully present in them both. For each one of us the moment of death is our personal equivalent of the black hole, falling into which we meet ourselves – and Christ. Without Christ death would be the ultimate annihilation, the collapse of the world into the state of No-God, which is sin – into which state when one falls the whole

## The Heart of the Mystery

of creation is sucked in behind. But we are never without Christ. Our very existence on this earth, attenuated and precarious as for the most part it seems to be, is the proof of this: we could not be sustained in the world of reality *at all* if it were not for the Divine Principle within us which upholds us (as the Angels were upheld as they joyfully capered on the needle's point). This is so because only in God are we capable of enduring the nothingness through which we must pass. God alone is able to overcome annihilation. Pinioned upon the black hole He sustains His Being in nothingness. So from Him the Rose springs forth. The Cross is encircled. Infinity becomes eternity. Man in Christ is saved.

This is one diagram of the Mystery. Another is contained in a painting by Velasquez in the Prado, which depicts the Assumption and Coronation of the Virgin. In it, the Father and the Son hold out a crown in the form of a jewelled circlet or ring. The Holy Dove descends from a point immediately above this ring as if to pass downwards through it. The Virgin rises upwards from beneath. It is as if She will pass upwards through the crown (like silk drawn through a ring) to be united with the Trinity in the moment of Her mystical identification with the descending Spirit. This is the final stage of the Mystery of Love: in the Myth it comes at the end. But we have to hold it in our minds from beginning to end. Indeed, the Creation story begins with the rising of Sophia (or Mary), the first creation, from the primal abyss (this is prior to the creation of Adam, which in Christian mythology is linked to the Fall of the Angels in a manner we shall presently elucidate). The Assumption of Mary is Her 'second' arising, the consummation of a cyclic movement of ascent and descent and ascent again. It represents the redemption of Creation, here identified with the Virgin, Who is Herself identified with Her Risen and Ascended Son. So Velasquez presents us with an image of the marriage of heaven and earth, the ultimate destiny of our world as it rises, embodied, into the Heart of God.

The Trinity is Movement. It is the Movement of the Godhead within Itself, movement in stillness.

Any meditation on the Trinity must start from the realisation that God is unknowable as He is in Himself. All the great religions teach us this. The Buddha refused even to speak of God at all. The Taoist scriptures leave us in no doubt:

> The Tao that can be named
> Is not the Everlasting Tao.

In the Christian tradition, the anonymous fourteenth-century treatise called the *Cloud of Unknowing* speaks of God as the naught of Whom no-thing can be known, approachable only through the cloud which represents the blinding of all the faculties of the soul of man. But then the great Sufi teacher Ibn' Arabi corrects this one-sided truth by putting these words into the mouth of God:

'I was a Hidden Treasure and I desired to be known.'

Love is a knowing and a being known; and God is Love: therefore He moves within Himself begetting the Beloved. In the first Movement of Love He knows Himself. This first Movement is the Trinity: God as Lover and Beloved and the Love which unites the two and is therefore continuously in motion between them: 'The Holy Spirit,' as it says in the Creed, 'proceeding from the Father and the Son'.

The Gnostics, in the early centuries of Christianity, spoke of the Holy Spirit as the Divine Sophia; and this is no mere 'heretical' identification but an old tradition which frequently reappears in the writings of the mystics; although at first sight we may feel there is little connection between the Third Person of the Trinity and the 'Sophia' of the Old Testament, even as the latter has been reinterpreted by the Church. 'Sophia' means 'Wisdom' and is feminine. The Divine Wisdom appears in the Book of Proverbs as She whom the Lord possessed 'in the beginning of his ways, before he made anything, from the beginning'. This passage has been incorporated into the Mass of the Immaculate Conception in the Roman Missal, so that Wisdom here becomes identified with Mary, the Mother of God. The lesson for the Feast includes these words:

'When he prepared the heavens I was there; when with a certain law and compass he enclosed the depths . . . when he balanced the foundations of the earth; I was with him, forming all things, and was delighted every day, playing before him at all

## The Heart of the Mystery

times, playing in the world: and my delight is to be with the children of men.'

The Mass of the Assumption likewise identifies Mary with the Divine Sophia, this time as She appears in the Book of Wisdom (which is not included in the Anglican Authorised Version of the Bible, but is accepted as canonical by Rome).

We are here confronted by one of the subtlest distinctions to be made by the Church in the process of developing the Myth. The Holy Spirit is in Himself Divine. Mary is Creation *deified* in Christ. There is, between these two Eternal Beings, the Spirit and the Virgin-who-becomes-the-Bride, a union which is in one sense a total identification, in another not. The Holy Spirit takes possession of Mary in such a way that She becomes Its embodiment. It has no other embodiment. This Mystery is hinted at in the Velasquez painting and again and again in the liturgy of the Church. It 'appears', as it were, twice in the linear 'story' of the Myth. It is there at the beginning; and then again at the end.

We must look first at the beginning:

'When he prepared the heavens I was there . . . playing before him at all times . . .'

But if Mary is, as the Church has consistently declared Her to be, a *created human being*, who is this?

## Chapter Three

# *In the Beginning*

'The Spirit of God moved upon the face of the waters . . .'

This is the 'second' movement of Love. Of this the Sufi poet Jalalu'l-Din Rumi writes:

'Thou didst contrive this "I" and "We" in order to play the game of worship with Thyself.'

For the sake of this 'game of love' (as so many of the mystics have ecstatically declared it to be) God made the Heavens and the earth.

But Man is the primary Creation. In Man is included all the worlds. Man was created in the image of God, to be the Mirror-Beloved of God, the created 'replica' of the Son. The Heavenly Virgin (or Sophia) is the first creation in the sense that, having been drawn up from and created out of the Void, She gives birth in Eternity to Man, the embodiment of celestial Light. Her primary uprising is associated with the coming-into-being of Lucifer, the Prince of Light. Lucifer is to be understood as the *Thought of Man in the Mind of God.*

Tradition associates Lucifer with the Second Person of the Trinity, the Divine Son.

This Divine Son is the 'only begotten'. He is God eternally begotten of God within Himself. The Creed contains a careful formulation of His Nature to insure against Its being confused with that of any created being, angelic or human, even with Christ Himself. No matter that Man is created in His image, and the Archangel Lucifer is the Thought-form of that image; no matter that He Himself became incarnate as a man: He remains *as He is in Himself* God, the Uncreated, as the Creed unambiguously declares Him to be: 'the Only-begotten Son of God, begotten of His Father before all worlds, God of God, Light of

## In the Beginning

Light, Very God of Very God, begotten not made, being of one substance with the Father by whom all things were made'.

The distinction lies, obviously, in the word 'made'. The Son is 'begotten' in the sense that in Him God knows Himself: the Father and the Son are 'of one substance'. It is this eternal, uncreated Son Who bestows a Form upon Created Man. In Man *something* is brought out of *nothing*. (Creation is, by definition, *ex nihilo* in the Christian tradition.) The initial movement of creation is the coming-into-being of a Divinely-created Thought. Lucifer is God's disembodied Thought. 'God said: Let there be Light. And there was Light.' Lucifer is the Prince of Light. He has form and luminosity but no embodiment. The Church has consistently taught that the Angels (of whom Lucifer is the original Archetype) are disembodied spirits. Man is a complex creation, an embodied spirit or spiritualised body. The Angels, we are told, are fashioned of a substance which is purely intellectual. This is by no means to say that they are 'ethereal' in the sense of being 'misty' and insubstantial in comparison with ourselves. The Angels are to be understood as representing the Eternal Ideas from which all created things arise. It is said that every individual human being, every species of animal and plant, every society, every nation, every race, has its own Angel who watches over it, representing what essentially it *is*, and what it is destined to *become*, guiding it along the Way which leads from its Divine Origin to its Divine End. Just as an artist begins with an idea, and embodies that idea in his work, so (in the Myth) did the Creator God. He began with the Angels and went on to embody their virtues in the forms of His created world. But something, according to the Myth, 'went wrong'.

Now, in this idea of something 'going wrong' we encounter the fundamental paradox at the root of the Christian tradition, the cause of its having been so frequently and so hopelessly misunderstood. We have to understand the Fall (which is the breaking up of the One into the many, the *realisation* of the principle of Evil in opposition to a lower form of the Good, no longer that absolute Wholeness which contains the principle of evil within Itself) as being at the same time inevitable and the outcome of a choice. We must even go further and see it as a Blessed Event. The Fall is the explanation of our 'world', the cause of God's action towards us in binding us to Him in the

## The Christian Mystery

Person of the Son: in this sense it was providential, foreseen, and a necessary part of the Movement of God's Love. But still it was brought into being by the exercise of the *freedom to deny*. God Himself is perfect Freedom. Love is not love unless it is freely and intentionally given, as a wholly disinterested offering for the sake of the Beloved, and with nothing held back. This implies the ability to refuse. God bestows upon His Creation this ability; since without it they could not love Him; and it is to love Him that they are made. 'Thou didst contrive this "I" and this "we" in order to play the game of worship with Thyself.'

In the Myth the Fall of Lucifer is prior to the Fall of Man. Lucifer falls on account of His Pride. He envies the Most High and desires to be as God. No lesser Angel could have desired such a thing. It is His supreme Beauty and Radiance which turns to His undoing. He plummets downwards into the Abyss, taking with Him those Angels who have elected to remain as His servants. At this point there is an ambiguity. We look for a logical, chronological story connecting the Luciferian Fall with the Creation; and there is none. The story of Lucifer is as much a part of the Christian tradition as the story of Adam and Eve; but the Genesis account of Creation does not mention it. Putting together the two stories, our conclusion must be that at some point, vaguely defined, *after* the Fall of the Angels, the world is created and Adam and Eve are put into it. They dwell in a state of innocence in the Paradise Garden. Tempted by Lucifer (now Satan) to imitate His original sin, they are banished from the Garden but do not, as He did, fall precipitately into Hell. It appears that they enter a wasteland, where they are still in communication with God, Who continues to care for them and will eventually save them from the consequences of their sin.

Attempts to interpret this story must always and of necessity be inadequate. While the Myth in its entirety has been interpreted for us by the mystics and by the early Fathers of the Church, assisted (as has already been pointed out) by many of the so-called 'heretics', these writers do not simply hand it to us, as it were, on a plate. Esoteric Christianity has seldom, if ever, been exposed in such a way that anyone and everyone can read about it and misunderstand it. It is there if we are able to understand. (Nowadays the situation is different: esotericism will have to be exposed, because there is an unprecedented

## In the Beginning

danger of its otherwise being lost.) In the end we shall find that even our 'expositions' are couched in mythological terms, *because it is only in those terms that we are able to comprehend metaphysical truth*. So what we are doing all the time is not so much 'explaining' the Myth as *compressing* it, in such a way as to bring out its meaning as a Timeless Event.

Lucifer is destined to preside over the coming-into-being of the Cosmic Man, the 'younger son' of the Creator God. This Man must be understood as being *all men* united in the One. He is at the same time the 'I' and the 'we' of the Sufi poet. Lucifer, as His Thought-form, arises in Eternity like the sun. In the same instant Sophia, the Feminine principle, is drawn up out of the Abyss to meet the descending Spirit. She is the Matrix or Womb from which Creation will come forth. When Lucifer falls, in His Pride, the Form of Man is shattered in the moment of its coming-into-existence. This may also be understood as the smashing of a *world*. Plato presents us with an extraordinary description of archetypal Man in the form of a *sphere*. This begins to seem less peculiar when we realise that the world itself – or more properly the 'worlds', since there are in reality innumerable interpenetrating worlds experienced by us according to the level on which we choose to live – are contained within Man. As Lucifer falls, the One breaks up into the many. Mankind as we know it appears – that is to say, ourselves. (This is leaving aside for the moment the story of Adam and Eve in their primal innocence, which has to be separately considered for reasons which will be explained in due course.) In this Angelic Fall the idea is suggested that it is not our bodies (as has often been supposed) but the angelic part of us, the pure flame of the spiritual intellect whereby we are enabled, if we choose, to apprehend the Divine, which brings about our undoing when we cease to remember that we are no-thing in God's Presence.

(We must never be misled into supposing that we have only to re-present the Myth in terms of our own day-to-day experience in order to 'understand' it. It does, however – for how could it not? – continuously illuminate every aspect of our lives. In the story of Lucifer, for instance, is to be found the answer to the question we so frequently find ourselves asking: If the acquisition of knowledge is a necessary part of our development socially and as individuals, at what point, if any, does our

## The Christian Mystery

knowledge overstep the bounds of the legitimate? At what point should we *stop*? Lucifer is Knowledge. He is the Prince of Light, the shining apparition of Intellectual Fire. But this does not mean that knowledge is of necessity Luciferian. Lucifer derives His knowledge from God; and that knowledge is re-offered to us in Christ. The answer to our question is that knowledge is legitimate in so far as it is balanced by humility. Originally – and we see this clearly in the Figure of Lucifer in the split instant of His existence before His Fall into the Abyss – Man was to be created as an intellectual being with the capacity to *know*. All knowledge was to be his divinely bestowed prerogative, save only the knowledge of the innermost Being of the Unknowable God. So man, in this 'half-way house' which is our world, may *know* in so far as he is willing to acknowledge that he is but a servant. It is not a question of *how much* we know, but of *how* we know it: in Lucifer the Proud Angel who willed to glorify *himself*, or in the Son of God.)

In the moment of His Fall Lucifer becomes Satan. In the same moment Sophia becomes Mary. Mary is the *human embodiment* of the Feminine principle, the Divine Sophia Who in Eternity 'plays before' the Lord. As Sophia is the *Womb of all life*, Mary is the *Womb of Salvation* Who gives birth to the Christ. She is frequently referred to as the Second Eve. A great deal has been made of the fact that the name 'Eva' is 'Ave' in reverse, suggesting that the Angelic salutation addresses the Virgin by Her own name and, in the same breath, by that of Her 'negative' counterpart, whose action is now to be *reversed*. But the Feminine principle is a Quaternary. There are 'Four Marys', if we may so put it. Sophia is the Origin of them all. The fourth member of the Quaternary is the Magdalen, the archetypal Prostitute. Our Velasquez painting of the Coronation of the Virgin-Bride depicts the re-union of the four Marys in the final episode of the Myth. This Mystery of Mary, which is situated at the very heart of Catholic Christianity, unfolds itself gradually to our understanding as we follow the story sequentially from beginning to end, remembering as we do so that the end is contained in the beginning, and the beginning in the end: the movement is cyclic; the 'story' revolves upon itself. Sophia, the Divine Wisdom, is the Crowned Virgin in Her Nuptials with the Son of God.

## Chapter Four

# *The Adam*

There is an ancient and widespread tradition that Man was originally androgyne. We find suggestions of this in certain apocryphal scriptures relating to Adam and Eve, in which the two of them together are referred to as 'the Adam'. Also, in the Book of Genesis, the two are split asunder in the moment of the drawing forth of the principle of Femininity, called Eve, which significantly occurs at a moment when the Adam is *asleep*. Sleep is a *forgetting*. In this episode it represents one aspect of the Fall: the loss of the primal integrity of the Perfect Man, which will have to be restored in a process of re-member-ance. The masculine principle is associated with Spirit and intellect; the feminine with Nature and soul: together they constitute our humanity.

The animals also, and indeed the entirety of the Paradise Garden, are to be understood as being contained within Man. That is why they fall with him. We are meant to understand that their present unhappy conditions, in which they prey upon one another and are preyed upon by men, came about, out of time, as a result of Man's sin. The Paradise Garden must be seen as the exteriorisation of Man in a state of Primal Innocence. He was driven out of it only in the sense that for him it ceased to exist: what came into existence in its place was the exteriorisation of his fallen state. Always 'the world' is simply Man: it belongs to him; it reflects him; it becomes his enemy only in the sense that he becomes an enemy to himself.

The Paradise Garden is the state of *Innocence*. It has to be separated out, as it were, from the story of Lucifer, from which it does not appear to follow on in what we would call a logical sequence of cause and effect. In it we see the 'split second' which occurs *after* the Luciferian Fall, and *before* the moment of Man's crucial choice. Lucifer was the Angel (or idea) of Cosmic Man. This semi-divine Being, had Lucifer not fallen, was destined to enjoy what in the Genesis story is described as 'the knowledge of Good and Evil', not as the conflict of two opposing principles but in the perfection of its Wholeness as the Vision of That which transcends the opposites. The story of the Adam suggests that Man, being himself free, was not compelled to follow his Angel but was given the alternative of remaining in a state of innocence, his 'right' to angelic knowledge forfeited by the Luciferian Fall but the possibility still open to him of remaining faithful and obedient to his Creator God. This possibility is represented in the story by the innocence and *ignorance* of the Adam before their personal act of disobedience in eating the forbidden fruit. The fruit itself is the Knowledge whereby God comprehends the Wholeness of the worlds. Grasped at by man, it instantaneously polarises itself. Evil is born into the world, standing over against an incomplete and lower 'Good'.

We cannot imagine a choice without a momentary state preceding that choice. The Paradise Garden is that momentary state. It does not preclude the idea that Man *in the instant of his creation* has to choose. He chooses between God and Lucifer; that is to say between God and the principle of egoistic pride within himself. We are not intended to deduce from the story that there can ever have been a *period of time* during which men and women existed in the state of the Adam in the Garden of Paradise. And, as the Myth unfolds itself, we shall see that Man achieves his eternal destiny mysteriously *through his sin*. It is the disobedience of the Adam which 'results' in the Incarnation of the Divine Son. God *intervenes*. Now *in Christ* man is once again permitted, and even commanded, to *know*. But before we go on to the central unfolding of the Myth we must linger for a while in this Garden, which (like Heaven and Hell, and like that other Garden in which we encounter the Risen Christ) is one of the innumerable interpenetrating 'worlds' of which our own is composed. Here in the Garden of Paradise we are in the place or 'world' of diffused and innocent joy in the beauty of Nature and the bounty of God's fruitful earth. Here is childlike, tender love; the warmth of sunshine and the coolness of a mountain spring. The seventeenth-century English mystic, Thomas Traherne,

## The Adam

appears to have had the extraordinary privilege of having been born in this state and remaining in it for several years before he was expelled from its delights:

The pure and unsullied perception I had from the womb and that divine light with which I was born are to this day the best in which I can see the universe. By the gift of God they attended me into this world and by his especial favour I remember them still. Everything appeared new and strange at first, inexpressibly rare, delightful and beautiful. I was a little stranger who at my entrance into the world was saluted and surrounded by innumerable joys. My knowledge was divine. I knew by intuition those things which since I have had to collect again by the highest reason. My very ignorance was advantageous. All things were spotless, pure and glorious, yes, and infinitely mine and joyful and precious. I did not know there were any sins or complaints or laws. I did not dream of poverty, strife or vices. All tears and quarrels were hidden from my eyes. Heaven and earth sang my Creator's praises. All time was eternity. The corn was radiant and immortal wheat which would never be replaced nor was ever sown. I thought it had stood everlastingly. The dust and stones of the street were as precious as gold. The gates were at first the end of the world. The green trees, when I saw them first through one of the gates, transported and ravished me. Their sweetness and unusual beauty made my heart leap. Men were like angels. Boys and girls tumbling in the street and playing were moving jewels. I did not know that they had been born and must die. The city seemed to stand in Eden or to be built in heaven; everything in it was mine. The skies, too, were mine and so were the sun and moon and stars. The whole world was mine and I alone looked at and enjoyed it. But with much trouble I was corrupted and made to learn the dirty devices of the world which I am now unlearning and becoming as it were a little child again, so that I may enter into the Kingdom of God.

Wordsworth wrote with the same moving sorrow of his own expulsion from the state of innocence:

## The Christian Mystery

> There was a time when meadow, grove and stream,
> The earth, and every common sight,
> To me did seem
> Apparelled in celestial light
> The glory and the freshness of a dream.
> It is not now as it has been of yore; –
> Turn wheresoe'er I may,
> By night or day,
> The things which I have seen I now can see no more.

The Adam were expelled from the Garden. The curse that was pronounced upon mankind, according to the story, is all the more terrible to read on account of its inescapable truth:

'Cursed is the ground for thy sake. Thorns and thistles shall it bring forth to thee . . . In the sweat of thy face shalt thou eat bread till thou return unto the ground; for out of it was thou taken: for dust thou art and unto dust shalt thou return.'

The meaning here is that man, having turned away from God, has cursed himself. His world has fallen with him, and has changed with the changes in him. At the same time we must recall once more that the 'cursed world' of the expulsion from Eden *is not to be identified wholly with our own*. Our world as we know it is held in a delicate balance between the opposites: fallen man is not wholly fallen after all; he is saved *in so far as he re-turns to God in Christ*.

The Adam, passing out of the Garden, enter into a 'state of waiting' which is neither 'this world' of our present experience nor the world of the utterly lost. It is what the Church calls 'Limbo'; and again it is a 'state' which we frequently experience. The *type* of the 'utterly lost' (and here we must stress the word 'type', because the Church has consistently taught that, while Hell is an eternal possibility, we are not to assume that any human being has ever fallen into it) is Judas Iscariot, as he appears in the Myth. The role of Judas, the Betrayer, is essential to a Drama in which all the possibilities open to mankind are eternally played out. We shall understand this better as the Myth unfolds. Meanwhile we refer to it only for the sake of pointing out that the story of the Adam is no more a representation of the Descent into Hell than it is of ourselves as we at present know ourselves to be. And now, at the risk of repetition, let us look again at this mystery of the state (or states) in which we *are*, and

## The Adam

see how it is to be related to those states which have been, as it were, *singled out of it* in the Myth.

'This world' is the state in which man hovers between acceptance and rejection of what, for want of a better figure of speech, we may call his 'second chance'. The Adam, in the person of their sinless Child, as She bows before Her destiny as the Mother of the Saving Christ, accept the salvation that is offered to them in the instant of the Fall, and are thereby *drawn back*. The Blessed Virgin Mary, being Herself sinless, is the Child of Sin in the sense of being directly descended from the original Two who lost themselves in Sin. These Two are refound in Her. Their Being coinheres in Hers, and in Hers is re-turned to God. That re-turning is the saving or salvation of mankind. In Eternity it *now is*. But *in time* it is *not yet*. Time has been *brought into being*; and time must be played out; the *fullness of time* must be accomplished *in us*. We resemble the world we inhabit, which is turning perpetually towards and away from the sun, poised between the darkness and the light. That is why in 'this world' Nature itself is ambivalent, so beautiful and so innocent and yet so relentless, smiting us with cancer at the same time as it ravishes us with its beauty and provides us with our daily bread and the water we drink. *Our world is that state in which mankind must exist until every single human soul has passed through the Cross into the New World which is our total incorporation into the Heavenly Church.*

The passing of this world into the Kingdom of God is not a process of change occurring in linear time. It is (as has already been pointed out) the fulfilment of time. It is, like the emergence of the dragonfly, a metamorphosis. It takes place 'in the twinkling of an eye'. But still it takes place *in this world* because it is *now*. It is *the present*. We do not live (for the most part) in the present. We meet it in death; and in moments of love, which themselves are a death for the ego-centred 'self'.

Each soul is required, separately, to *choose*. This is what we are all of us waiting for, here in a world which is *held* by the saving action of the Cross in a momentary equilibrium between the opposites, balanced between the evil and the good. Nature remains beautiful in this state; because beauty is equilibrium, order, harmony and balance, the working out of everlasting laws – even when those laws are maintained, as they must be in our world, at the price of blood and under the necessity of death. Nature is innocent, 'for the creature was made subject to vanity not willingly'. It is not the fault either of the animals or of our animal nature that our spiritual pride has condemned them and us to the conditions under which we are forced to exist. St Paul tells us this; and he further points out that the creatures 'groaning and travailing in pain together until now await the redemption of the sons of God'. We wait for each other; and the animals wait patiently for us, because they are mysteriously *contained in us*, and must follow us wherever we take them, for better or for worse.

It is emphasised in the story that the Adam must *toil*. It is only through the acquisition of *knowledge* that man is enabled to overcome the harshness of his 'natural' existence in continuous struggle with the elements. So here again we find the idea that knowledge is either *Luciferian* (and so, since the Fall, forbidden) or *Christian* in the sense of being received and used within the Mystical Body of Christ which is the Universal Church. And because this world is, by definition, neither the Kingdom of Heaven nor the wasteland of the exiled Adam, but the drawing out in time of the point where we choose between the two, its conditions will not alter *in time* in any permanent or radical sense, no matter how frenziedly we strive to obtain for ourselves the maximum of ease and the minimum of pain: the balance must be constantly maintained, and that balance will continuously readjust itself. If this seems hard, we chose it. The Christian Mystery is nothing if not hard: if we try to soften it, we lose its meaning; if we find it unattractive we may look elsewhere, and find that the other great religions, in their various ways, are equally hard. In the rhythms of the Christian year we are given our holy-days or holidays, our quota of happiness and rest. As for joy, it is ours for the asking all the time. God is our joy. But we have to accept the conditions of *where we are* before we can avail ourselves of that heavenly comfort.

The Adam put themselves in Limbo. Christ, in His redemptive action, offers us a 'way out'. This world is that way; or it can be. It is both the way out of Limbo and the way in. The Adam, we are given to understand, repented of their disobedience. Even so, the Garden of their Innocence was for ever gone. The Garden of the Resurrection was still to come. They found themselves in the wasteland; but there stretched before them the prospect of making a new kind of garden, the garden of 'this world' and of time, where the flowers bloom and fruit and die and rise again, on and on and on in the seemingly endless cycles of life and death. So Adam is three times over a gardener: first in Eden, tending a garden which burgeoned in orderly profusion beneath his lightest touch; second in 'this world'; and third in the Person of Christ, the 'Second Adam' whom Mary Magdalen 'mistook' for the gardener in the Resurrection Garden, where the Rose blossoms eternally out of the forsaken tomb.

The story of the Adam may be read, of course, from many points of view. We can see it as an interpretation of the process of 'evolution', showing that man-in-a-state-of-nature or *natural* man was originally 'intended' to evolve in harmonious obedience to the laws of God, until he was *ready* to be raised from the status of a servant to that of a Son. This moment of 'readiness' would have corresponded to his identification with his Angel, Lucifer, his Heavenly Counterpart; for Lucifer, had He *not* fallen, would have functioned as the means of drawing man *upwards* towards God. It has to be understood that the Myth is so rich that we never come to the end of 'interpreting' it; and each new 'interpretation' will fit in consistently with the rest, provided we remember that we are dealing *not* with a 'logical' *allegory*, but with a network of images corresponding to every level of a multidimensional truth. These images can be comprehended by us only in so far as we contemplate them in silence – that is to say humbly, without arguing in terms of our own 'logic' with the beautiful integrity of the Myth, which holds together as it does so many meanings within itself.

## Chapter Five

# *The Mystery of Sin*

Julian of Norwich, the fourteenth-century anchoress, wrote of sin:

'Sin is behovely. But all shall be well, and all manner thing shall be well.'

And T. S. Eliot, in his *Four Quartets*, which contain so many quotations from the mystics, adds this to her words:

> When the tongues of flame are enfolded
> Into the crowned knot of fire
> And the Fire and the Rose are One.

The Myth teaches us to be thankful for 'all manner thing', even for sin. There is no understanding the story of the Paradise Garden until we are able *at the same time* to feel its horrendousness, and see that it is not there to teach us what we 'ought' and 'ought not' to do, but to show us how a purely innocent and childlike state, radiantly beautiful as it is, is not to be compared to the glory which is to be revealed, the fulfilled and consummated glory of the Sons of God. Instinctively, by the simple and unlettered, as by the mystics, this has always been understood. In the heyday of the Middle Ages, that time above all others when the Church was hellbent upon terrifying men and women with visions of eternal punishment, the people sang:

> Adam lay i-bowndyn
> bowndyn in a bond,
> Fowre thousand wynter
> thowt he not to long;

## The Mystery of Sin

And al was for an appil,
    an appil that he tok,
As clerkes fyndyn wretyn
    in her Book.

Ne hadde the appil take ben,
    the appil taken ben,
Ne hadde never our lady
    a ben hevene quen.

Blyssid be the tyme
    that appil taken was!
Therefore we mown syngn
    Deo gracias!

In the story of the Garden there are three primary sins. These three are pride, disobedience and lust. (The last of the three is suggested merely, by the fact that the Adam suddenly discover themselves to be naked and are ashamed of their nakedness.) It is interesting that the sin of murder, arising out of envy and typifying 'man's inhumanity to man', comes later (in the story of Cain and Abel, Adam's sons) and is presented as an inevitable consequence of the other three. The actual eating of the 'appil' is an act of disobedience arising out of pride. Pride comes first of all. Pride is the sin of Lucifer, or that part of us which constitutes our spiritual and intellectual endowment; disobedience and lust are sins of the 'natural' man, who, like the Adam, is misled by the higher part of himself, and becomes a passive rather than an active agent in his own collapse. The serpent (who is, of course, Lucifer or Satan) says to the Adam: 'Ye shall not surely die: for God doth know that in the day ye eat thereof, then your eyes shall be opened, and ye shall be as gods.'

The 'eating' here refers to the acquisition of a particular *kind* of knowledge – that of 'good' and 'evil' as opposing principles, split asunder in the Luciferian Fall and so for ever destructive of the state of innocence. This knowledge has been forbidden to mankind, here seen as existing in its post-Luciferian but *pre-Christian* state. Pride enters the heart of the Adam and they *disobey* God's command. (It is worth noticing here that later, in the context of the Mystical Church, there is no further mention of 'commands': the 'new law' which is instituted by Christ is not one of 'commands' but of Love.)

## The Christian Mystery

The Lord God had commanded the Adam:

'Of every tree in the garden thou mayest freely eat, but of the tree of the Knowledge of Good and Evil thou shalt not eat of it; for in the day that thou eatest thereof thou shalt surely die.'

This is the opposite of the promise of the serpent. The tempter holds out the prospect of a self-sufficient immortality based upon knowledge and achievement. He lies. Again and again in the writings of the Christian tradition, Satan is described as the Liar; and, if we wish to find the prototype of this particular sin, we may look here: not at the Adam and their children, but at the Evil One Himself.

The three primary sins of the Adam represent the inversion of the three primary gifts bestowed by the Creator upon Lucifer because they were intended for Man: Knowledge, Freedom, Ecstasy; the power to *know*, the power to *do*, and the power to *create*. These three powers are attributes of God. In attributing them to himself as if they were *his own* Man turns them into their opposites. Prompted by the deceiving serpent, who is intellectual pride, the Adam acquire the gifts that were originally to be theirs, but acquire them *in the wrong way*. And they do not, after all, become 'as gods'. Pride, disobedience and lust are forms of enslavement. The Adam, in refusing to be *servants*, become *slaves*. Had they consented to be servants, the Myth implies, they would have found themselves raised into being sons (and they will still be so raised; but now at the price of blood and on the other side of death): refusing, they find themselves degraded into being slaves not of God (Who has no slaves) but of themselves.

Knowledge, Freedom, Ecstasy – mysteriously, it is these primary gifts which actually *bring about* the Luciferian Fall. The attributes of the Godhead are 'too much' for the creature, whether that creature be an Angel or a man. Tradition suggests that God, in His Eternal Omniscience, foresaw this; but could not withhold His gifts, because in the Act of Creation He was giving Himself. So God saw that He Himself must be crucified by sin. This is the 'measure' of the Love of God which is without measure. 'I was a Hidden Treasure; and I desired to be known.' *This was the only way it could be done.* The Christian Mystery invites us to contemplate this unfathomable Act, whereby we were created to be something more than we, of ourselves, are able to endure and continue to exist; so that God, in creating us,

## The Mystery of Sin

intervenes and preserves us in the moment of our extinction by uniting us to Him in Christ.

We are baffled altogether by the Mystery of Sin. However we think of it there is paradox. On the one hand, we feel shame; on the other we see inevitability, and beyond inevitability even joy, in the accomplishment of a higher good. On the one hand, we know that already in Eternity, which is Now, we are with Christ; on the other we are conscious of wandering in a half-lit world where we seem to be sinning in our sleep. Very few of the great spiritual teachers have attempted to 'explain' these paradoxes to us in such a way that we can grasp them with our finite minds. Julian of Norwich was one of those who struggled ardently both to understand them herself and to help others to understand. She was the recipient of a series of metaphysical revelations in which she was totally reassured of the Mercy of God. 'Thou shalt see for thyself', it was said to her again and again, 'that all shall be well.'

Julian had been excruciatingly perplexed because, as she explains to us, Holy church and her own conscience had taught her the heinousness of sin; and yet in all her visions she saw nothing but God's love as if there were no sin.

'Yet in this I wondered and pondered with all the diligence of my soul, after this fashion: Good Lord, I see thee – that thou art very truth; and I know truly that we sin grievously all day, and are most blameworthy. I cannot evade the knowledge of this truth, yet I see not thee shewing to us any manner of blame. How may this be?'

Her perplexity increased until in desperation she besought the Lord God to reveal to her the mystery of sin, adding with endearing humility that she was made bold to ask because 'it is so low a thing – for if it were an high, I should be afraid to ask it'. Whereupon 'our courteous Lord answered in shewing full mistily a wonderful parable of a Lord that hath a servant'.

This parable constitutes the fifty-first and longest chapter of Julian's *Revelations of Divine Love*, and should be read in full by anyone who desires to share in her enlightenment. It describes how the servant stands meekly before the Lord, who sends him on an errand 'to do that which was his will' and to fetch 'a treasure on the earth which the Lord loved'.

'The servant not only goeth, but starteth out suddenly, and

runneth in great haste, for love to do his Lord's will. But straightway he falleth down into a ravine, and taketh full great hurt; and then he groaneth and moaneth, waileth and turneth about, but he cannot rise or help himself in any manner. In all this, the most misfortune that I saw him in was failing of comfort; for he could not turn his face to look upon his loving Lord.' Julian goes on to enumerate his sufferings. 'I marvelled', she says, 'how the servant could thus meekly suffer all this woe. And I beheld with deliberation to discover if I could perceive in him any fault; or whether the Lord would assign to him any kind of blame. And truly there was none seen; for his good will and his great desire were the only cause of his falling.'

Gradually it turns out that the servant represents in some mysterious manner both the Adam *and* the Christ.

> The servant that stood before him, I understood that he was shewed for Adam: that is to say, one man was shewed, in the time of his falling. For in the sight of God every man is one man, and one man is every-man. This man was hurt in his powers, and made full feeble; and he was stunned in his understanding, in that he was turned from the beholding of his Lord. But his will was preserved in God's sight; for his will I saw our Lord commend and approve. But he himself was hindered and blinded in the knowing of his true will; which is the cause to him of great sorrow and grievous distress. For he neither seeth clearly his loving Lord, who is full meek and mild towards him; nor seeth he truly how he himself is in the sight of his loving Lord. And well I wot, when these two be wisely and truly seen, we shall get rest and peace, in part here, and their fullness in bliss, in heaven: by his plenteous grace.

This passage appears at first glance entirely to deny the reality of sin. Julian is forever on the verge of doing this; but she resolves the paradox by joining together the twin images of the Adam falling into sin and the Son of God falling into the Virgin's womb:

> In the servant is comprehended the second person of the Trinity. And in the servant is comprehended Adam: that is to say every-man. Thus when I say 'the son', this meaneth the

## The Mystery of Sin

Godhead which is equal to the Father's; and when I say 'the servant', it meaneth Christ's manhood which is the true Adam . . . The Lord is God the Father; the servant is the son Jesus Christ. The Holy Ghost is the equal love which is in them both. When Adam fell, God's Son fell; because of the true oneing which was made in heaven, God's son could not be separated from Adam. (By Adam I understand every-man.) Adam fell from life to death into the deeps of this wretched world, and after that into hell. God's Son fell, with Adam, into the deeps of the Maiden's womb, who was the fairest daughter of Adam; and that, for to excuse Adam from blame in heaven and earth; and mightily he fetched him out of hell . . . For in all this our good Lord shewed his own Son and Adam as one man.

Of this 'marvellous parable' Julian says that she has 'teaching within me as it were the beginning of an ABC'. Even as she presents and explains it, it is far from easy to understand; but its beauty and clarity are so extraordinary that we accept it as being the nearest approximation to a full explanation that we are entitled to expect. The above are short extracts only from a long chapter which spills over into another which still further expounds its contents: indeed, one could justly say that the whole of Julian's book is an exposition of that one 'shewing', since the whole book is concerned with a revelation of how God, in the Incarnation, responds to man's sin with an access of Divine Love. Her theme is that of the carol which lauds not Adam's sin but the Divine reaction whereby Christ was identified with that sin: 'Blyssid be the tyme that appil taken was!'

For *now* is God in man and man in God. Even in the bondage of time we may know this; and know also that when we are freed from the bondage of time its full meaning will become apparent:

'Beloved, now are we the sons of God; and it doth not yet appear what we shall be.'

St Paul, who wrote those words, was far from being unconscious of his own habit of falling into sins. Like Julian, he seems to have felt that this mattered and did not matter, both at once. The Christian Mystery is a blinding paradox. That is why, down the centuries, it has only been acceptable on the one hand

## The Christian Mystery

to the mystics, on the other to the simple and unlearned who have taken it in the form of stories, visual images, and practical instructions for its application to their everyday lives. The merely learned have never understood; the merely 'clever' still less. It is these, not the illiterate, who have had to be ordered to obey. That is why the Church has traditionally upheld the principle that learning is actually bad for a great many people, and should be the prerogative of those who are capable of understanding what they learn. This is not, in our world, a principle which can be enforced without abuse. In our world there are no solutions. This characteristic of our world is, for Christians, not only an empirical fact but a metaphysical truth.

In passing we may remind ourselves that Julian's revelation is not, of course, exclusively Christian. There is a Sufic saying, for instance: 'Each thing hath two faces, a face of its own, and a face of its Lord; in respect of its own face it is nothingness, and in respect of the Face of God it is Being.' These are the two faces of Julian's 'servant'.

Chapter Six

# *The Word Made Flesh*

The opening paragraph of the Gospel of St John has generally been regarded as an exposition of the mystical meaning of Christianity, which is of course above all else the religion of the Incarnation of God.

'In the beginning was the Word . . . and the Word was made flesh.'

There is no need to delay ourselves here with a general investigation of the meaning of the term *Logos* or 'Word' in the Ancient World, from which St John (or whoever wrote his gospel) borrowed it. In Christian terminology, it refers to the Second Person of the Trinity, Who is defined by it as the Eternal Utterance of the First. We may visualise it, if we choose, as the infinite expansion of a single syllable into space. The Hindu scriptures refer to this syllable as the sound OM or AUM. The Breath of Brahma, they tell us, creates the worlds and dissolves them again, as it flows forever in and out, filling the illimitable Void and then emptying it again, as the aeons pass and Eternity folds back upon Itself. The Christian tradition expresses the same idea in terms of Ascent and Descent. Its Myth is a diagram based upon this theme. The Descent of the Word is Creation, the Spirit descending upon Mary, the descent into Hell which takes place between the Crucifixion and the Resurrection and represents the actual moment of Christ's death. In this descent the Word is made flesh. In the liturgy of the Catholic Church there are three separate points at which, for centuries, the faithful sank momentarily to their knees. These were during the Creed at the words 'And was made man'; in the Last Gospel at the words 'And the Word was made flesh'; and during the solemn reading of the Passion at the words 'He gave up the ghost'. In each case the gesture was one of humility and awe before the infinite condescension of God in taking upon Himself the nature of man and submitting to the necessity of death.

The Word became flesh as the means of reconciling fallen humanity to God. That is to say He *falls with man*, so that man may be enabled to rise again with Him. The idea of being 'made flesh' has to do with the Fall. The Christian tradition distinguishes between *the body*, which is intrinsically holy, and what we have been accustomed to calling *matter*, which is the principle of density and weight. The Resurrection-body is characterised by *lightness*. (The double use of the word 'light' in the English language is interesting, because it is a question of the same thing seen from two different points of view.) We are inclined to think of this 'lightness' as implying a kind of mistiness and ethereality; with the result that we look at the Resurrection stories the wrong way round, assuming that the Christ-body passed through locked doors and solid walls because it had the properties of a 'ghost'. But this Christ-body of the Resurrection is the true substance, compared with which we ourselves are like dreams walking. Speaking of that substance, as it manifests itself in the Divine Wisdom, the scriptures tell us: 'She passeth and goeth through all things by reason of her pureness.'

The Christ-body of the Resurrection has arisen from the tomb of matter and begun the process of Its reascent. It is still a *body*, one with, yet eternally distinct from, the Holy Spirit of God, Who bore It *as seed* into the Virgin's womb. It can assume, but is no longer subject to, weight. It has form and substance: indeed It is the perfection of form and the plenitude of substance. Weight is another matter; or rather, weight is the definition of what we have always called 'matter'. Nowadays we are learning a new language from the physicists; but the former usage was accurate to express what was then being talked about. The principle of materiality is *dense* and *drags down*. It is opposed to the principle of spirituality, which is light and transparent. By the one we fall; by the other we rise. These are metaphysical ideas; and we need not confuse our minds by attempting to transpose them into the language of contemporary scientific research. A time may come when the two languages can be brought together and properly synchronised to enable us to appreciate the validity of both.

Simone Weil has provided us with a key to the ambivalent

## The Word Made Flesh

character of our bodily nature in her concept of 'gravity and grace'. She contrasts the density of matter with the purity of spirit, showing how Nature, including our bodies, is poised between the two. Even the stones possess a concealed fire and are capable of manifesting 'light'. At a higher level, in the plant, the same principle of spirituality manifests itself as beauty of form and vibrancy of life. Its opposite has frequently been symbolised by the formlessness and density of the rock which was imagined to be at the centre of the earth. (This may well have been an unconscious realisation of the possibility of the black hole: an image in contemporary terms of light trapped in density and darkness beyond the possibility of escape.) The 'Limbo' into which Christ descends in search of men's souls has traditionally been represented as a region of compressed rock in which the souls are entrapped. Persephone was dragged down by the Ruler of Hades into a similar realm. It is hardly surprising that the Cathars, reacting against the fearful materialism of the medieval Church – which itself had to do with the notion that all things material had been sanctified by Christ and might therefore be conveniently enjoyed by His servants – asserted that it was blasphemy to suggest that God Himself could be born, suffer, and die 'in the flesh'. Rather than admit such a seeming contradiction, they maintained that the Christ-nature descended upon the man Jesus at His baptism, and departed before the Crucifixion to avoid becoming contaminated by bodily pain. Persecuted, tortured, and finally massacred by the 'orthodox', they represent a point of view which has proved to be ineradicable, because it is one side of a delicately paradoxical truth.

The Gnostics in general, of whom the Cathars represent an extremist offshoot, tended in the direction of this 'immaterialist' viewpoint. In common with Plato and Plotinus, they looked upon the body as a kind of trap. The spirit, they said, was imprisoned in matter and awaiting its release. The story of the Descent into Limbo expresses the same idea: properly understood, Christianity, far from denying this idea, elucidates it, showing how the spiritualised body rises out of the realm of 'gravity' into that of 'grace'. St Paul, who was virtually the founder of 'orthodoxy', himself declared: 'The Kingdom of God cannot be enjoyed by flesh and blood', adding in explanation that 'the principle of corruption cannot share a life which is incorruptible'.

An Orphic fragment which has come down to us in isolation from its context provides one of the most beautiful descriptions in the literature of mysticism of our spiritual nature released in the moment of death:

> Thou shalt find to the left of the House of Hades a spring, and by the side thereof standing a white cypress. To this spring approach not near.
>
> But thou shalt find another, from the Lake of Memory, cold water flowing forth and there are guardians before it. Say:
>
> 'I am the child of Earth and Starry Heaven, but my race is of Heaven alone. This ye know yourselves. But I am parched with thirst and I perish. Give me quickly the cold water flowing forth from the Lake of Memory.'

'Memory' here seems to refer to the spiritual home of the disembodied soul before its fall into the density of the material world. In the Apocryphal Acts of Judas Thomas the Apostle there occurs a marvellous parable on the same theme. The Apostle is arrested in India and flung into prison. 'And while he was praying, all those who were in prison saw that he was praying, and begged of him to pray for them too. And when he had prayed and sat down, Judas began to chant this hymn.' Reading it, we cannot doubt the interpretation given by the translator in his introduction: 'We have here an ancient Gnostic hymn relating to the Soul, which is sent from its heavenly home to the earth, and there forgets both its origin and its mission until it is aroused by a revelation from on high; thereupon it performs the task assigned to it and returns to the upper regions, where it is reunited to the heavenly robe, its ideal counterpart, and enters into the presence of the highest celestial Powers.' The hymn begins:

> When I was a little child
> And dwelling in my Kingdom in my Father's house,
>
> And in the wealth and the glories
> of my nurturers had my pleasure,

## The Word Made Flesh

> From the East, our home,
> My parents, having equipped me, sent me forth.

The East is, traditionally, the direction of the spiritual world. The 'I' of the hymn, who is clearly identical with Julian's 'servant', is sent in the opposite direction to fetch one precious pearl 'which is in the midst of the sea, hard by the loud-breathing serpent'.

> And they took off from me the bright robe
> which in their love they had wrought for me,
>
> And my purple toga,
> which was measured and woven to my stature.
>
> And they made a compact with me . . .

The compact is that when he fetches back the pearl, his 'bright robe' and toga will be restored. So he goes down into Egypt (in the Jewish and Christian traditions, the land of exile), 'single and alone, a stranger to those with whom I dwelt'.

> And I put on a garb like theirs,
> Lest they should insult me because I had come from afar,
> To take away the pearl . . .

Julian's 'servant', too, was sent out to fetch a treasure, with the result that he fell into a ditch. In the Hymn of Judas Thomas, the Soul or the Son of God (for clearly, as with Julian, the image is a double one, signifying both) eats the food of the Egyptians, reminding us of Persephone and the seed of the pomegranate, and of how again and again in the mythology of the world the captive is warned not to eat of the alien food – for we become what we eat.

> I forgot that I was a Son of Kings,
> And I forgot the pearl . . .

The pearl is, like Julian's treasure, another image of the soul to be redeemed by Christ. In mystical parables of this order it is useless to expect the kind of straightforward allegory in which A equals B, and the images do not elude us by shifting about. We might find this easier to 'understand', but it would not illuminate our hearts.

> But all these things that befell me
> My parents perceived and were grieved for me . . .
> And they wrote to me a letter. . .

> Up and arise from thy sleep!
> Think of thy bright robe,
> And remember thy glorious toga,
> Which thou shalt put on as thine adornment.

The letter 'flew in the likeness of an eagle' and alighted beside him. He read it.

> And according to what was traced in my heart
> Were the words of my letter written.

> I remembered that I was a son of Kings . . .

So he begins to charm the serpent who guards the pearl, hushing him to sleep:

> For my Father's name I named over him,
> And the name of our next in rank,
> And of my Mother, the Queen of the East . . .

The naming of the Elder Brother (with whom, however, he is in a certain sense identified) reminds us of the parable of the Prodigal Son. When the pearl has been achieved, the letter leads him home, shining before him.

> And with his love was drawing me on . . .

His parents send their treasures with his bright robe and his toga.

> And because I remembered not its fashion
> For in my childhood I had left it in my Father's house

## *The Word Made Flesh*

> On a sudden as I faced it
> The garment seemed to me like a mirror of myself.
>
> I saw it all in my whole self,
> Moreover I faced my whole self in facing it.
>
> For we were two in distinction
> And yet again one in likeness . . .

The soul returns to his Father's house, where his Father rejoices over him as in that other and very similar parable told by Jesus. It is typical of this kind of story, which has to be read in many different ways and on many levels at once, that the Father both is and is *not* to be identified with God Himself.

> And he promised that also to the gate
> Of the King of Kings I should speed with him,
>
> And bringing my gift and my pearl
> I should appear with him before our King.

The Father *was* 'the King'. But there is, after all, a still higher King. In the literature of mysticism we find this idea again and again. On every level of being there is, as it were, a Representative of God.

## Chapter Seven

# *The Mystery of the Virgin*

Mary is Sophia, the Matrix of Creation, the Mother of Man, the Bride of God. She is Christ's mother on earth, because He is the Son of Man. But in Heaven She is His Bride, because in Heaven the Church, in the person of Mary, is eternally united to the Son. Christ and the Mystical Church are the Masculine and Feminine principles of Creation. This Mystical Church, which tradition and the liturgy identifies with Mary, is an image of mankind redeemed; it is All Souls in Christ. The shocking doctrine – shocking because from the first it was so perversely and deliberately misunderstood – *Extra Ecclesiam nulla salus* ('outside the Church is no salvation') is a perfectly legitimate way of expressing this *mythological* truth. The Church in this sense is all men everywhere who seek the face of God. And Mary is the Church.

In the Myth there is a splitting asunder of the Feminine principle in the instant of the Fall. Eve (or Eva, to give her the Latinised form of her name, of which so much has been made as the 'reversal' of the Angelic salutation) becomes at the same time the mother and the temptress of the fallen human race. Mary too is our Mother (the image of 'motherhood' in 'our world', like that of femininity itself, is bewilderingly ambivalent). And Mary too is the Lover of mankind. This is the Mystery of the two Marys of the New Testament: Mary the Mother of Jesus and Mary the archetypal prostitute. Of the latter we shall have more to say in the proper place; but it needs to be explained at once that she appears in the story as a prostitute because it belongs to the essential nature of Mary to be the lover of 'all mankind'. 'All men' in Eternity coinhere in the Divine Bridegroom, Who is Christ. But 'all men' in the Fall are scattered and separate. So

## The Mystery of the Virgin

this Mary is a prostitute because, until she encounters the Christ, she cannot be anything else. And yet prostitution is a sin. Her sin is 'undone' when she *recognises* her True Love. This 'aspect' of Mary is one of the 'hidden' mysteries which are guarded by the Church. It is deeply paradoxical; whereas in the figure of the Virgin we behold quite simply the Divine Purity in human form. Purity is one of the Attributes of God. In Islam these Attributes are spoken of as the Divine Names. In Hinduism and in many other religions they are personified as gods and goddesses. God Himself is the Plenitude of all His Attributes, and transcends them all.

Mary, who is to be the Mother of Jesus, is the untouched vessel prepared from all eternity to receive the Divine Seed which 'falls' from above to fructify the barren earth. The Church has called Her the God-bearer. This title refers not only to the actual birth of Christ, but suggests that She bears Her Divine Child in Her arms to present Him to the world, as a torch-bearer carries a light. For this cause She was set apart. Her inviolate sanctity, as She awaits the unfolding of Her unique vocation, makes Her, humanly speaking, the loneliest figure of all time. She arises in Eternity as the Immaculate Conception: single and self-contained, opening out like a perfect flower to God. Her symbol is the lily, the pure white single-petalled blossom with the golden sceptre rising from its heart. (Only in the final phase of Her glorification does She become the Mystic Rose: as Virgin, She is not yet Bride. Mary the Virgin and Mary Magdalen are individualised figures until the End of the Story or the end of time.) Another image which has been employed to represent Her is that of the spotless mirror which so perfectly reflects the sun that it appears to be itself a 'second sun'. Another is the translucent wineglass, so pure that it becomes invisible, as if turned into the wine which fills it. The doctrine of the Immaculate Conception, which declares that Mary was conceived in Her mother's womb without the inherited taint of Adam's sin, is the logical corollary of Her function as the containing principle which, being filled with the Spirit of God, can contain nothing else. '. . . therefore shall no defiled thing fall into her.' Perfect Purity is perfect passibility. Nothing that is impure, nothing that is not God, can linger in it for an instant.

In all this Mary is unlike Her Son. The world cannot touch

Her. He descends into the depths of matter, is crushed by the forces of 'gravity', wounded, humiliated, besmirched, subjected to the final ignominy of death. The Virgin remains beautiful to the end, and does not die but falls asleep. The doctrine of the Immaculate Conception involves the idea that the Virgin was redeemed, as it were 'in advance', by the atoning Passion of the Cross. Devout Catholics have asked how this could be. The question is unanswerable for those who are unable to let go of the concept of linear time. The teaching itself is essential to an understanding of what the Virgin represents. She alone of all creation does not *fall*, because in the instant of Her conception She is upheld by the saving Action of Her Son. The Immaculate Conception is the moment of the coming-into-being of redeemed humanity, the Mystical Church.

In the apocryphal Gospel of Mary, traditionally ascribed to St James and known as the Protovangelion, we read of her earthly conception as a semimiraculous event. The story is a familiar one: the births of Isaac and of Samuel are among the best known examples of the type, which is met with all over the world in innumerable fairy-tales and myths. Anna and Joachim are a devout, elderly couple who have given up hope of a child. An Angelic Messenger reassures them, separately, that Anna will shortly conceive. They hasten to meet each other at the city gate. 'And she ran, and hanging about his neck said, Now I know that the Lord hath greatly blessed me.' In the many pictorial representations of this meeting, the gate appears prominently in the background, symbolising unmistakably the vaginal passage to the womb. The elderly couple are shown embracing one another with a loving kiss. The doctrine of the Immaculate Conception in no way depends upon, or implies, the idea that Mary was not conceived in the normal manner as a result of the sexual act: there is, however, a tradition identifying her conception with the meeting at the Golden Gate and with the kiss exchanged between her parents. In the literature of Christian mysticism the kiss appears frequently as symbolising the union between the soul and Christ.

When she is three years old the child is taken to the temple by her parents, and entrusted to the high priest. As with Isaac and Samuel, the manner of her birth has suggested to them that the Lord requires her to be set apart. She is not theirs but His. 'And

## The Mystery of the Virgin

the high priest received her and blessed her . . . and he placed her upon the third step of the altar and the Lord gave her grace and she danced with her feet.' Dancing, in all the traditions, symbolises the creation and restoration of the worlds. So she, who will be the instrument of the Redemption, and was with the Creator in the beginning, 'playing before him' and delighting in His works, dances before Him as a human child on His altar steps. 'And all the house of Israel loved her. And her parents went away filled with wonder and praising God.'

Mary remained in the temple until she was twelve years old. Then, because it would have been against the Law for her to continue living there after she began to menstruate, the priests decided to marry her to a man who would respect her virginity and protect it. The story is reminiscent of innumerable fairy-tales in which the hand of the princess is reserved for the one who can pass the appointed test. In this case the assembled suitors are presented with rods; and 'the last rod was taken by Joseph, and behold a dove proceeded out of the rod'. Joseph, in the Protovangelion, is a builder. He leaves Mary in his house, where she occupies herself with spinning the purple thread for the temple veil. As she sits alone and spins, we are reminded again of the fairy-tales; but this time it is not a sinister old woman who comes in.

> And the Angel of the Lord appeared unto Mary
> And she conceived by the Holy Ghost.

There is no more marvellous scene than this engraved upon the minds of men. It is majestic and pathetic both at once. The mighty Archangel bathed in the light of heaven, face to face with the fourteen-year-old girl, who is scared but not out of her wits, as she tremulously questions what He says. 'Hail thou that art highly favoured, the Lord is with thee; blessed art thou among women . . . and behold thou shalt conceive in thy womb and bear a son . . .' The Angel has said it, but 'How can this be seeing that I know not a man?' She takes her virginity for granted; there is no question of its ever being broken by Joseph or anyone else; even an Archangel cannot be telling her that. Mythology and fairy-tale teem with occasions when a question is expected to be asked: it is absolutely necessary; without it the drama is unable to proceed and everything must return to its starting point in the hope that 'next time round' it will work itself out. The actor must remember his role. Mary, having been allotted the leading part, remembers hers. She asks the right question, the cue for the Angel to obtain from her an act of pure consent.

'The Holy Ghost shall come upon thee and the power of the Most High shall overshadow thee: therefore also that holy thing which shall be born of thee shall be called the Son of God . . . for with God nothing is impossible.'

Will she believe in this reassurance? Will she indeed be reassured by it, and not draw back in terror from such a prospect?

> And Mary said,
> Behold the handmaid of the Lord;
> Be it unto me according to thy word.

This is one of the key passages of the New Testament. The heart of the Christian Mystery is contained in it. There is no redemption without consent. Mary consents to her function on behalf of the entirety of the human race.

As so often, it is a medieval carol which perfectly expresses, in simple language, the 'feel' of this scene:

> I sing of a maiden
> that is makeless
> King of all kings
> to her son she ches.

The words 'she ches' are typical of the metaphysical accuracy of even the simplest songs in an age of faith. The carol goes on:

> He came al so stille
> wher his moder was
> as dew in April
> that falleth on grass.

The Annunciation, like Easter, is celebrated at the vernal equinox. Christian art most frequently represents it by the two figures of Our Lady and St Gabriel, sometimes with a prayer

## The Mystery of the Virgin

desk and the upright lily in a jar, often with a window opening out of the cool, dim room (symbol of the Virgin's womb) upon a garden bathed in the light of early morning and of spring. Crivelli, however, painted it as taking place in the midst of the world. His great Annunciation in the National Gallery is set in a palace, the courtyards of which are scintillating with life, courtiers and children, animals and birds, flowers and fruits; and through it all on a straight strong shaft direct from God the winged Spirit bearing the Divine Seed, eternity piercing time, splitting time asunder in an instant by the power of the heavenly grace. *Ave Maria gratia plena*: 'Hail Mary full of grace . . .'

The Descent of the Spirit at the Annunciation is that Holy Event which makes possible the Immaculate Conception of the Virgin Herself. In the instant of Her own conception in her mother's womb She is upheld by the descending Spirit. She could not have been born as she is had she not consented in eternity to be the bearer of the Christ. That, if we can accept it, is the answer to the question of how She was redeemed from the beginning by an event which, in the chronological sequence of the Myth, had not yet taken place. These two events, the conception of the Virgin and that of the Eternal Word in the womb of the Virgin, take place simultaneously, outside time, together with that 'other' descent of the Spirit at Pentecost, which represents the founding of the Church. Nor is this all. If we think about it, there are two other 'occasions' of a similar kind; and we can see without too much difficulty how they too exist and are conjoined upon the same dimensionless point. In the opening chapter of Genesis the Spirit descends upon the face of the waters, and brings forth life. Here, the 'waters' represent both the primal ocean which stirs in the abyss and renders up the worlds and the watery matrix of the womb, Mary's womb and the womb of every woman since time began. Finally there is the scene of the Baptism, in which the Spirit descends upon Jesus as He rises from the water, born again 'of water and the spirit', and is acknowledged by a Voice from Heaven as being the Son of God.

Chapter Eight

# *The Mystery of St John*

It is easy not to notice the familiar words with which St Luke's account of the Annunciation begins: '*And in the sixth month* the Angel Gabriel was sent from God'.

The 'sixth month' refers to the pregnancy of Mary's cousin Elizabeth, and so to John the Baptist who was six months older than Jesus. The three stories – of the birth of Jesus and of Mary and of John – are mysteriously woven together in the various accounts of them, canonical and otherwise, which tradition has preserved and artists have reflected in their work.

The experiences of Anna (or St Anne) and her husband are almost exactly similar to those of Elizabeth and Zacharias, except that Zacharias is unable to believe in the Angelic promise and is struck dumb as a punishment. (Had Joachim refused to believe, would the birth have been that of the Baptist instead of the Mother of Christ; and is it this eternal possibility, this necessity of *waiting* from one to another of the cycles of time, that the Baptist represents?) Zacharias is the high priest. The Protovangelion implies that his encounter with the Angel follows immediately after his bestowal upon Mary of the purple thread to be spun *while she waits*. Therefore she is spinning for six months, from the time of the conception of the Baptist to that of her own son Jesus. Spinning is traditionally a symbol of time in its function as the instrument of destiny or Providence. One cannot avoid the conclusion that Mary's spinning is intended to be linked in some way to the formation of the Baptist in his mother's womb. The destinies of these two children, Mary's and Elizabeth's, are so intimately involved the one with the other that there seems, at times, to be a near-identification between the two. In Christian art, the personal insignia of John the Baptist is the *Agnus Dei*, the Lamb of God, which represents the Christ. He carries this Lamb; while supporting, in the crook of his other arm, a long cross identical with the one which is carried by the Lamb whenever It is depicted by Itself.

Mary, having been told by the Angel of Elizabeth's miraculous pregnancy, immediately pays her a visit. The Mystery (and we should note that the Church habitually refers to it as such) of the Visitation is depicted in Christian iconography as the moment of their meeting in a fond embrace. This reminds us of the meeting of Anna and Joachim at the gate; and it is in its own way a life-bestowing encounter of a similar sort. There is something extraordinarily touching and human about it; but the moment contains, as it were, an extra dimension; it points to a reality beyond itself. John the Baptist is the only saint in the Church's calender whose feast day is celebrated on his birthday rather than on the anniversary of his death. For all but this one of the saints, sanctification is a process extending through life and reaching its fulfilment in the moment when the soul is received into the Presence of God. John the Baptist is considered to have been sanctified in his mother's womb. As Mary embraces Elizabeth, the latter exclaims: 'When the voice of thy salutation was heard in mine ears the babe leaped in my womb for joy.' John is *born* in a state of sanctity, as a consequence of his prenatal encounter with the infant Jesus.

Unexpectedly, considering the significance attached to this birth, its portrayal in Christian art is relatively infrequent. Where it does appear, the subject is virtually indistinguishable from that of the birth of the Virgin to St Anne. There is between Elizabeth and Anne a bond of near-identification not dissimilar to that which exists between Christ and St John. A familiar Renaissance 'Holy Family' consists of the Virgin, her mother and the two small boys. Elizabeth is not present. Anne, whose story is so similar, *is* Elizabeth. Rudolph Steiner, whose unusual visions of the Mysteries were the outcome of certain private visionary experiences of his own, gives a highly complicated explanation of these paintings, in which he maintains that there were in reality two Jesus-children, this being a 'hidden' teaching known to such artists as Raphael and Leonardo because they were initiates of an esoteric School. Steiner was nothing if not an 'odd man out'. But he exemplifies, in his own way, that preoccupation with the Mystery of St John which characterised the Cathars, the Knights Templar and many another 'gnostic' sect whose 'unorthodoxy' was relentlessly condemned.

An old tradition associates John the Baptist with the Spiritual Sun. All over the Ancient World the visible sun was held to be the manifestation of an omnipresent divinity, the principle of Light and Life. The striking resemblance between many of the ancient representations of the Sun God and traditional Christian paintings of the head of the Baptist seen against the background of the 'platter' on which it was carried to the King, reinforce this association; as does the fact that his feast day coincides with the summer solstice, and is celebrated with customs derived from sun-worship. But Christ too, and Christ above all, was the Spiritual Sun. He supplanted for Christians the *Sol Invictus* of Mithraism; and meanwhile it is said that, for certain groups or cells within the main body of the Church, the Baptist was the *old sun* which must die every year and be supplanted by the new. Hence his title of the 'Forerunner', suggesting one who has trodden the way *before*, 'making the path straight'; hence too that strange saying in reference to the new Lord: 'He must increase; I must decrease.' The Feast of the Nativity of St John the Baptist celebrates the 'split second' of the sun's zenith before it begins to die. The Feast of the Nativity of Jesus, closely followed by that of the other St John (which is neither the anniversary of his birth nor of his death, because it is said that he did not die but has fallen asleep until the Last Day), occurs at the midwinter solstice, the moment when, the solar death having been accomplished, the new sun is born. Always, in myth, the same name implies an identification of some sort. And in fact it is the second St John whose even more intimate association with Jesus has been of absorbing interest to the Christian gnostics, beyond that of the first.

The Mystery of the two St Johns is connected with role playing and with cycles of time. It is perhaps the most 'hidden' of all the esoteric aspects of the Myth; so much so that we can never hope to understand it, and must be content with hints. Rodney Collin, whom many regard as the most profound thinker of the Gurdjieff-Ouspensky School (like J. G. Bennett, who emerged from the same School, he became a Roman Catholic), suggests that the Beloved Disciple was 'understudying' the Christ. This is

## The Mystery of St John

a reference to the idea that Jesus was playing out a Cosmic Drama in which 'next time round' there will be a general shifting of roles because this Jesus, having 'played' the Christ, will have passed into a higher sphere of existence. (From this point of view, we can see how Jesus and the two St Johns together form a trilogy of 'suns', the Past and the Future on either side of the Present. In this 'picture', however, we have to understand that the Baptist is not the One Who previously 'played' the Christ; but the one who, on this turn of the spiral, steps into His vacant place. These things are mysteries too dark for us; but it is as well to realise that such ideas exist and have been taught.) Other writers have drawn attention to the parallel between the second St John, of whom Jesus said that 'he shall tarry till I come', and Ananda, the 'beloved disciple' of the Buddha, who is said to be sleeping in a cave, awaiting the coming of the New Buddha at the end of this cycle of time. The Parousia or Second Coming of the Christ is paralleled in this Myth of the Maitreya Buddha whose appearance will inaugurate the reign of Love. Is Ananda himself the Maitreya, that he must not die, but await the moment of 'coming again'?

In St John the Beloved Disciple, Christ loves, as it were, an image of Himself. The love between these two is chaste but not sexless: its homosexual character is obvious to everyone but the 'orthodox'. Whether we like it or not, there is a constantly recurring suggestion in the esoteric literature of the world that homosexual love between men is the highest form of human relationship provided it is not physically expressed. Plato and Socrates taught this. The love between Christ and St John is the supreme image, in human terms, of the Love with which God Loves Himself. It is balanced by the love between Christ and the Magdalen. According to a little-known but significant tradition, the marriage at Cana was between Mary Magdalen and St John. This represents the idea that in Heaven (where the 'water' of this world becomes the 'wine' of the next) all our loves are united in the Love of God.

Finally we may recall an old legend concerning this second St John. It relates how he departed from this world at the age of ninety-nine. Gathering his disciples about him, he repeated again and again: 'My children, love one another.' Then he caused a grave to be dug beneath the altar and descended into it, praying; there to be enveloped like the phoenix in a blinding light and fire in the midst of which he disappeared. Afterwards the grave was found to be filled with manna which gave forth a heavenly fragrance. Manna is the 'bread from heaven', type of the Body of Christ. This then was all that was left of the transmuted body of the Beloved.

## Chapter Nine

# *The Mysteries of the Infant Christ*

*Christus Natus Est!*

The essence of it is surprise, a cry in the dark of infinite, almost unendurable delight. First comes Advent, the four weeks of darkness and cold when the great Antiphons ring out, calling for the Lord to come: 'O Wisdom . . . O Adonai . . . O Dayspring'. And then:

'When all things were in quiet silence and the night was in the midst of her course thy Almighty Word O Lord leapt down from Heaven from thy royal throne . . .'

There is no other day in the whole cycle of the year which has the magic of Christmas Day. The New Light appears as a tiny point of fire at midnight at the winter solstice. At the Mysteries of Eleusis the cry was heard: 'Holy Brimo has borne the Holy Child Brimos!' But the celebration goes back and back, beyond Eleusis, deep into the prehistory of mankind; and before the appearance of man it was celebrated by the earth itself, as the cycles of nature reflected it: *Hodie Christus Natus Est!*

The world has teemed throughout its history with half-divine, half-human saviour gods. Gods of fertility, gods of the sun. Their stories parallel that of the Christ, so many closely related expressions of the same truth. Tammuz, Osiris, Attis, Dionysos, Adonis, Mithras – to name but a few is misleading, for there are so many that their names could be chanted for an hour or more. In innumerable instances these divinities are *born in caves*. The cave is the mouth of Hades or Limbo; it leads downwards to the centre of the earth. It is the mouth of the womb. In one version of the Christian Nativity the Saviour's birthplace is a cave, and this is important because it relates His birthplace to the tomb, and reveals a correspondence between Joseph the husband of Mary and Joseph of Arimathea. The latter, having recently purchased a cave-tomb for the reception of his own body, gives it up to the body of the Lord, just as the former renounces his rights over the womb of his newly-wedded wife.

However, in the canonical and more familiar version the birthplace is a stable; and this image, although there is no mention in the Gospels of 'the ox and the ass', has given rise to the tradition that it took place in the presence of the beasts of the field, man's humble servants. Mary and Joseph, having been summarily turned away by worldly men, are received by two gentle, harmless creatures who represent a mysterious category of the animal world. The beasts of burden have been half-redeemed, half-victimised by men. One can see their destiny from either point of view; it is one manifestation of the constant ambivalence of 'this world', in which men are sometimes merciful, sometimes merciless, to each other and to their fellow creatures for whom they must answer to God. The ox and the ass participate in man's punishment, whereby he must eat bread 'in the sweat of his face'. They are stupid beasts; and somehow this very stupidity is their passport to Christ. Stupid, harmless, faithful, innocent even of the bloodshedding which nature itself forces upon wild animals in a fallen world, they stand in silent adoration breathing down upon the Incarnate Word. One cannot so easily imagine a wild animal, or a strikingly beautiful animal, or a sharply intelligent animal, being accorded the supreme privilege that was bestowed upon the ox and the ass. *O Magnum Mysterium et admirabile Sacramentum ut animalia viderent dominum natum iacentem in praesepio.*

The Nativity scene has been familiarised for us in the Christmas Crib. This in its simplest form consists of Mary and Joseph and the babe, with the ox and the ass, an angel in the background representing the multitudes of the heavenly host. The shepherds have not yet arrived. Innocent animality and pure spirituality have been present at the holy birth, which itself has been a 'miraculous' event. An ancient prayer attributed to St Ephraem refers in no uncertain manner to the doctrine of Mary's perpetual virginity as this has been consistently defined by the Church. It is not always realised how uncompromising this doctrine is:

## The Mysteries of the Infant Christ

'Golden censer, brightest of lamps, fairest vessel filled with heavenly manna, tablet inscribed with the divine commandments . . . thou hast brought forth God and man, yet art virgin still, after as before his birth. He turned not the key of that Eastern gateway; it remains forever shut . . .'

In cruder terms, the hymen remained unbroken. Our Lady is addressed as *Beata Maria semper virgine*, Blessed Mary Evervirgin, in one after another of the Church's litanies and prayers. Details of the holy birth are withheld. Of the Buddha we are told that He was born from His mother's side while she clung to the branch of a flowering tree. But the birth of the Christ is a mystery too holy to be described. There is something about the whole atmosphere of Christmas which is not so much awesome (for it is after all the homeliest of feasts) as so intimate and so beautiful that we cover our faces and shed tears in the presence of the Godhead so strangely and wonderfully descended to earth. It is partly on account of this quality of almost unendurable poignancy that only very simple people are able to enter the presence of the newborn Christ: the sophisticated would be totally overthrown, not knowing how to react to such an experience.

> The Shepherds on the Lawn,
> Or ere the point of dawn,
>   Sate simply chatting in a rustic row . . .
> Perhaps their loves or else their sheep
> Was all that did their silly thoughts so busie keep.
>
> When such music sweet
> Their hearts and ears did greet,
>   As never was by mortall finger strook . . .

Nowadays we are a little inclined to wince at this description of the poor 'rustics' and their 'silly thoughts'. But, whether we like it or not (and we had better learn to like it if we want to understand what Christianity has to teach) illiteracy has not been held to be a great misfortune by the Church. On the contrary, it is the quality of simple-mindedness, so hard for the learned to rediscover, that the Christian tradition has consistently extolled. The shepherds received the Good News before the Kings. The Wise Men had to travel a long way; but the shepherds hurried on foot a short distance, and came to the stable 'and found Mary and Joseph and the Babe lying in a manger'.

By the time the Kings appear, the Holy Family have left the stable (or cave) and are living in a house. These Three Kings (or Wise Men) are the knowing ones, the powerful ones, those who are rich in worldly experience as well as in worldly goods. Their visit is celebrated on the 'twelfth day of Christmas' as the Feast of the Epiphany. On this day, it is said, the Holy Child is 'shown' to the world. The Three Kings 'came from afar'. Their coming represents the completion of the Nativity, in the sense that the Light which came into being as a dimensionless point has expanded and is now a world-including sphere; the circumference and the centre have been oned in the process of this journey; infinitude has burst into luminosity; time itself has been fulfilled. Invariably one of the Kings is depicted as a very old man: he comes from the beginning of time. The star which they follow is the tiny light of the newborn child leading them into the centre along a spiralling way, shining in darkness. Theirs is the first and archetypal pilgrimage. Entering wholly into 'this world', they lose sight of the star; but 'this world' itself (represented by the court of the evil King) contains signs and prophecies of the Kingdom of God. On the last stage of their journey they rely upon these signs. Afterwards they must return 'another way'. Their pilgrimage has led them in a double spiral within *and* around a multidimensional globe, tracing out the path of one of the greater cycles or aeons of time (represented in the Church's year by the 'twelve days'). If this figure is hard to imagine, we must try at least to realise that the End of the Journey is situated not only at the centre but on every point of the circumference. Traditionally, one direction of the spiral is 'right', the other 'wrong'. When one reaches the end there is a momentary hiatus; one cycle is over, another is about to begin: one must not 'return the same way'.

The Three Kings bring gifts. This is an awesome Mystery. It tells us that God does not demand anything from us as tribute. The Kings themselves levy tribute from their subjects. But Christ the King is revealed to them as a helpless child who is not in a position to demand anything from them as a right. The world can be returned to Him only in the form of a gift. They kneel before Him and offer it. The 'three gifts' have innumerable meanings. Traditionally, it has always been said that the gold signifies worldly riches and power (it is also knowledge, on account of its association with the light of the sun); the frankincense is prayer and praise (it is also the delights of the senses, the fragrance of the beautiful); and the myrrh is sorrow. Sorrow seems a strange gift; but the gift of the world inevitably includes it.

The visit of the Three Kings leads on to the story of the Flight. The Holy Child must be *hidden* from the fury of 'the world'. Here we encounter the idea that a point of light, in the first instant of its coming-to-be, is invisible. It is infinitely small. The darkness appears to engulf it. Further, the Myth implies that the darkness is enormously powerful. If the light were *not* hidden it would actually be put out. In the story of the Flight of the Holy Family into Egypt, Herod, the evil King, has ordered the death of the Child. When He cannot be found, the order is extended. Now every male child 'of two years old and under' must be slain on the chance that one of them may be the Christ. So an act of substitution is performed. The Holy Babe is preserved; while the 'Holy Innocents', who represent an infinite number of *replicas* of the Babe, are murdered in His place.

The Holy Innocents are the 'types' of the Child Jesus. In all the great world religions we come upon the idea, presented in one form or another, of the breaking up of the One into the many, resulting in a proliferation of 'types' – depicted, for instance, in the painted banners (called *t'ankas*) of Tibetan Buddhism as row upon row of tiny identical Bodhisattvas or Lamist saints; and again as the myriad heads of the Lord Chenrezig, whose head 'burst into a thousand fragments' in pity for the sufferings of the world. The Lord Chenrezig craved permission of His Divine Father to go down into the world of men for the sake of all beings until all could be freed from the bondage of ignorance. The story presents an exact parallel to that of the Christ. There are of course innumerable others. Every man is a 'type' or replica of the One. The story of the Innocents is a particular version of this idea, a myth within a Myth. Its peculiarity consists in the perfect *innocence* of the murdered babes. The original shattering of Creation in the Fall produces, if not annihilation, at least (in the 'half-way' world) a proliferation of 'types' that are grievously *flawed* and await restoration by their 'anti-type', the Son of God,

## The Christian Mystery

Who descends from Heaven on their behalf. The Innocents have *already been* restored. They typify the idea that in Christ we are all of us *made innocent*. In Him we are as Julian's 'servant', who fell and was not condemned. But this can only be so in so far as we *die* in Him and are 'baptised' in the moment of death.

Babies (like lambs) have always been regarded as *symbolising* the Divine Innocence. Christianity does not teach that they *are* innocent. On the contrary, we are told that the entirety of mankind, with the exception of the Virgin, is involved in Adam's sin, in the sense that each one of us in eternity has a part in committing that sin. The story of the Holy Innocents has to do with this idea. It is hard for us to understand this story – hard in the obvious sense, at the exoteric level where we question the morality of saving one child at the expense of so many who must die in its place; and harder still when we are asked to understand what this actually *means* in terms of our encounter with the Justice and the Mercy of God.

Whether we like it or not, the entire mythology of the world presents us with the idea that we shall live eternally *only* by consenting to die, and *only* by the sacrifice of 'blood' (which signifies the principle of life, alike on the level of the body and of the spirit). The Christian Myth has emphasised the *justice* of our predicament, since we brought it upon ourselves. In Adam we disobeyed God. This disobedience was the forfeiting – or *murder* – of our primal innocence. The tradition that the Garden of Paradise was submerged in a river of blood is a variation on the theme of the murdered babes. The blood is the life-blood of mankind. Humanity (as in the story of Cain and Abel) slays itself. But the blood of all-men coinheres in the Life of the Godhead bestowed upon us by Christ. One tiny 'drop' of this Divine Life introduced into the bloodstream of mankind transforms that stream into a cleansing flood. In that flood the 'Holy Innocents' are *baptised*. The blood of their sacrifice (and we are left in no doubt of the horrible bloodiness of their deaths) is not theirs only, it is His, transformed in the mystery of reciprocal Substitution which is the innermost meaning of the Cross.

The Sacrament of Baptism by *water* is, so to speak, an incomplete image of the restoration of the world in Christ. It is *His* blood-sacrifice which makes possible the restoration of our

## The Mysteries of the Infant Christ

state of innocence by means of *water*, which signifies repentance. 'Water' is *our side* of the transaction. But, as the water is turned into wine (in the story of the Marriage at Cana) and the wine into blood in the Eucharistic rite, so we must in the end pass through death; and the water of our baptism is transformed into the Blood of the Divine Sacrifice. So the Church has always taught that those early martyrs for the Faith who died 'unbaptised' (with water) were not in reality so, because they received 'the baptism of blood'. Again, in the First World War, when a strange mood of exultation was abroad, it was said (on both sides) that 'the fallen' would 'go straight to Heaven', this being an unconsciously produced version of the same myth. The Holy Infants, having received this baptism in the instant of their coming-to-be (the *simultaneity* of the Fall, the Nativity, and the Flight is implicit in the Myth), are truly and perfectly innocent. In 'this world' the state of innocence is impossible to *maintain*. But these children die in the same instant as they are *born* and *baptised* (more surely perhaps than with any other episode in the Myth, we should try to see this one as not having an extension in time). IN THE SIMULTANEITY OF ETERNITY EVENTS AFFECT THEIR OWN CAUSES, AND ARE CAUSED BY THEIR OWN EFFECTS. The story of the Holy Innocents is an exceptionally clear and beautiful example of this truth.

The Divine Son is assailed in the moment of His Descent. The Inviolable is violated; His Perfect Form is shattered and scattered in the Six Directions; and yet He remains intact: through the web of those myriad forms He, who is the archetype of them all, is enabled to escape. He escapes for the duration of a cycle of time. At the end of that cycle, in the prime of His earthly existence (traditionally, Jesus was thirty-three years old at the time of His death), He will again be destroyed, this time as the Divine Victim, the Substitute for the entirety of mankind 'made innocent' in Him. This 'second time' He will not 'escape'; He will rise in triumph from the dead. Christ is the Beginning and the End. In the Beginning He is the Archetypal Child. In His Aspect as Light He is a pinpoint star, dimensionless, infinitely vulnerable to the encroaching dark. So others must be substituted for Him. If the One is to be given for the many, the many must 'first' die for the One. (This does *not* mean, of course, that their deaths are, in reality, prior to His. The One Archetypal

## The Christian Mystery

Sacrifice is that of God Himself.) In the deaths of the Holy Innocents everything in the Christ-nature that is capable of destruction is destroyed, instantaneously slain by the impact of an alien substance – human sin. But His Holy Essence slips through the meshes of that death; and in doing so draws back Its types into Itself, to await the Resurrection into Everlasting Life.

Always the Innocents are represented as being cut in pieces by the sword. They are wrenched, undefended, from their mothers' arms. The significance of 'the sword' as the instrument of their Passion is that it is, supremely, the weapon which can *hack in pieces* and *draw blood*. In the many Christian paintings of this subject, the mothers are never depicted as being physically injured in defending their children: indeed they do not even attempt to defend them. They are types of the Virgin, to whom it was said in the temple when She presented Her Son: 'Yea, a sword shall pierce thine own soul also'. That 'also' refers to the mothers of the murdered babes. The Blessed Virgin is physically invulnerable. But the sword which pierces Her Son's body will pierce Her soul with anguish at the foot of the Cross.

Chapter Ten

# The Ministry of Jesus

At this point we need to remind ourselves again that the Lord Jesus was *playing a role*. The Jesus of history – the Jesus, that is to say, who appeared on our own particular line of historical time – was speaking and acting as the representative upon earth *at that time* of the One in Whom His personal identity had been totally offered up. His personal biography thus became a *tracing* of the Myth.

This happens, to a greater or a lesser extent, in the case of all those who pattern themselves consciously upon an eternal archetype. There have been, in the history of the world, certain individuals of whom tradition declares that they came down from heaven. Others have so closely patterned themselves upon one or other of these that a virtual identification has been achieved, as in the case of St Francis, whose body was marked with the wounds of the Christ. In the life histories of these exceptional men and women certain peculiar similarities appear, as if they were reproducing imperfectly, in time, a series of Divine Events. This phenomenon can never have been more clearly marked than as we see it exemplified in the historical Jesus. Yet we do not know *precisely* to what extent it applied even to Him.

A number of historical figures have been, since their deaths, appropriated entirely by myth. King Arthur is an obvious instance. We tend to forget that there may be historical characters hidden behind the stories of Krishna, Osiris, Dionysos and many another of the gods. The biography of Jesus does not fall into this category, since the one we possess is apparently *more or less* historically accurate, at least as regards the time between the commencement of His ministry and His death. But the Church, as it formulated and ritualised one of the greatest versions of the Universal Myth ever to appear in the history of mankind, inevitably disregarded the kind of factual accuracy of historical detail which *to us* seems so important. We seldom realise the extent to which our present-day society is obsessed with 'history' and with 'facts'. Not so long ago this obsession would have been incomprehensible to virtually the entirety of the human race. Even in the Middle Ages, when the idea was a new and heady intoxication for the learned, few people would have understood it. The authors of the Gospels, even in those parts of their narratives which deal with day-to-day events and report the sayings of Jesus, would not have been troubled by typical present-day scruples about handing on stories which had previously been passed down from one disciple to another by word of mouth. Of this, however, we may be sure: the Lord Jesus understood His own role; He knew what He was doing, and His instructed disciples and those who were instructed by them also knew. *That* is what the Gospels are about. They are records of *that*. In reading them, we may be sure that, regardless of what is 'historical' and what is not, we shall not be misled by a word, if what we are in search of is not 'history' but truth.

Returning then to our search, we find that the childhood of Jesus, from the time of the Flight into Egypt until He reaches the age of twelve, is passed over in silence by the Evangelists. (Not so the apocryphal gospels, which indulge in a number of stories, most of them rather unattractive from an exoteric point of view.) The age of twelve is the threshold of maturity. It is the end of a small cycle within the larger cycle of a person's life. There is a pause; and an unwinding. Jesus unwinds, at this point, the ties which have bound Him to His parents. A fifteenth-century painting by the Italian artist Butinone depicts Him seated at the apex of a spiral surrounded by the learned doctors of the temple. The story relates how He gave His parents 'the slip' in Jerusalem, and was eventually found by them in the temple 'seated in the midst of the doctors, hearing them and asking them questions'. This is the beginning of His schooling. He returns home for a while; and again the Evangelists fall silent. But we have the persistent tradition that He went into the desert to live with the sect of the Essenes, who represented the 'gnostic' element in the Judaism of that time. He must have had teachers.

## The Ministry of Jesus

He must have been instructed by someone in the inwardness of the Jewish tradition to which He belonged; and one cannot avoid the conclusion that He joined an Esoteric School which guided its disciples along an initiatic path.

We first encounter the mature Jesus when He steps out to be baptised in the Jordan by His cousin John. John has already declared to his own disciples that there is a higher baptism than the one he is empowered to confer: 'I indeed baptise you with water,' he has said to them, 'but He that cometh after me is mightier than I. He shall baptise you with the Holy Spirit and with fire.' An initiate may pass on to others only that which he himself has already received. So Jesus, after receiving the baptism of John, steps out of the water and is immediately baptised 'with fire' from above. The Holy Spirit descends upon Him and a Voice from Heaven declares Him to be the Son of God.

Apparent in the few hints we receive relating to the ministry of John is the concept of that ministry being a 'lower level' or 'pre-Christian' administration, which encounters the Mystical Church as the apex of an ascending pyramid might touch its descending counterpart. The point of contact is the Baptism of Jesus. Jesus is initiated into the Mysteries of John, so that John may be initiated into the Mysteries of the Christ. (The idea of the 'Greater' and the 'Lesser' Mysteries was widespread and already of great antiquity.) Shortly after this Event, John's initiation is confirmed. He receives the 'Baptism of Blood', when his head is cut off and carried on a circular platter (symbolising the disc of the expiring sun) to be presented to the 'evil King'. Fire, blood, wine – all these are images of the Divine Life which comes down from above. Sometimes, too, they can be images of a corresponding force which *rises* from the world of men, as if returning to its Source. In many traditions, beheading signifies the release of colossal forces as the life-blood spurts upwards and the vital energies escape. The Baptist must pass on to Jesus the accumulated spiritual energies of the 'level' upon which he himself operates, and which he, in a unique manner, represents. In return, not only he but the entirety of that which coinheres in him will receive the Fire from above. Again there is a substitution. The Baptism of Jesus and the Decapitation of John are two aspects of a single Event. Separated in time, they meet in

## The Christian Mystery

Eternity upon a point. That point is the meeting-place of two complementary streams of power. The one comes directly from Heaven. The other is the total and willing surrender of all the lower levels of existence. Jesus, in the exercise of His ministry, requires both. He fuses the two.

At this point we find Him surrounding Himself with an intimate circle, His chosen 'twelve'. The sun symbolism is again apparent, twelve being the number of the zodiacal signs. Instances in Christian and pre-Christian mythology of the band of twelve followers corresponding to the zodiacal band are of common occurrence, an obvious example being that of King Arthur and his knights. The twelve apostles represent twelve 'rays' or 'signs' or 'aspects' of the Christ. One of these is a ray of darkness; one of the apostles is Judas. Judas will be permitted to play his part and will then be replaced. The Round Table of the Upper Room has one chair which must be temporarily vacated and then occupied by someone else. The Mystery of Judas is something which the Church has never encouraged anyone to contemplate. Instinctively we turn away from it. Who are we to understand the meaning of irredeemable sin? Many people have demanded to be permitted to love Judas. To them one can only point out that there is no one and nothing there to be loved; unless, perhaps, in the depths of the Mystery, in search of the lost Judas we may find that Christ Himself is standing in his place.

The Ministry of Jesus was to be very short; and He must have been aware of this. It was to be a provocation to the world. Preparing for it by a period of forty days' prayer and fasting in the desert, He rejects the world's values on three levels – physical, psychical and spiritual:

> And when the tempter came to him he said, If thou be the Son of God command that these stones be made bread . . . Then the devil taketh him up into the holy city and setteth him on a pinnacle of the temple, and saith unto him, if thou be the Son of God cast thyself down . . . Again the devil showeth him all the kingdoms of the world and the glory of them and saith unto him, All these things will I give thee if thou wilt fall down and worship me.

## The Ministry of Jesus

These three temptations represent the three levels in an obvious sense: again, if we look more deeply, each temptation can be read in a way which covers all three. Jesus, having summarily rebuked the Devil, emerges from the desert and begins to preach. He preaches the gospel of the Fatherhood of God. In none of the four Gospels do we find Him expounding in plain language (if such a thing be possible) the Mystery of the Birth and Death and Resurrection of the Christ. We do not know in what terms He interpreted this Mystery to Himself. Like the Buddha and St Francis and the Tibetan Milarepa and many others known and unknown to us, who modelled their lives upon a Celestial Archetype, He must have known Himself to be identified with One who was greater than the man Jesus; but He does not explain this to the crowds: and the Evangelists do not explain it to us. Their readers are *expected to know*. The Gospel of St John is by far the most explicit; but all four read like documents which were written for the purpose of conveying in veiled language truths which would only be understood by those who had received previous instruction to enable them to understand. The Mystery was not, at that time, to be made public. Even in the ages of Faith, it was shrouded in symbolism and myth, the inner meaning of which was never publicly explained: only in our own strange times, on account of an unprecedented situation, is it necessary to spell out in so many words what up till now has been intentionally concealed. If Jesus had stood up before the people and proclaimed Himself in His cosmic role, they might have acclaimed Him as their king but they would not have understood, and the result would have been a blasphemous falsification of the truth. What he actually did was to show them the way of life of the children of God.

He did this by example and by word of mouth. He stressed again and again that the greatest of all the commandments is the first, which bids us to love God. God is our Father in Heaven; and we should love one another because we are all of us His children. The teachings of Jesus are totally uncompromising. He enjoins upon all who follow Him a kind of absolute generosity in giving, forgiving, availability, charity and forgetfulness of self. He tells His followers to live completely in the 'now', trusting in the providence (or provide-ence) of God. He says that the things of this world do not matter in the least. Jesus despised security.

He derided with abusive and picturesque epithets the complacency of the 'establishment'. When it suited His purposes to do so, He broke the Law, and then pointed out scornfully that laws were made for men's good and should be interpreted by common sense. He spoke violently and strangely about the punishments in store for those who rejected His message of humility and love. It was no easy message to accept; but He made no allowances for that.

The gospel accounts of the Ministry are divided between straight teaching, parables, healings and other 'miracles', and a number of disconnected episodes, most of which are encounters between Jesus and various members of the public: a rich young man, a supercilious host at a party, a prostitute. In St John's gospel, two of these encounters are used to communicate some of the more profound and esoteric teachings given by Jesus to His more intimate circle of friends. These two are with Nicodemus and with the woman at the well. The former takes place by night; the latter at noon. The polarisation appears to be intentional. To Nicodemus He speaks of the necessity of being 'born again'. This is a reference to the baptism which is higher than that of John; or rather to the inner meaning of that baptism; it is necessary, Jesus says, to be born not only of the flesh but of 'water and the Spirit'. In answer to the Pharisee's puzzled questions, He comes nearer than at any other point in the written records to explaining *Himself*. 'For God so loved the world', He says, 'that He gave His only begotten Son, that whosoever believeth in Him, should not perish, but have everlasting life.' The whole discourse is concerned with the light that 'shineth in darkness'. 'Light is come into the world, and men loved darkness rather than light . . . but he that doeth truth cometh to the light.' Light in darkness; birth out of the womb of the world into the freedom of the Spirit – this is the theme of the meeting by night.

Nicodemus, a Pharisee, is a representative of tradition and the Jewish Law. Shortly after this encounter, Jesus meets the woman of Samaria, an 'outsider' from the point of view of the Jews, a woman – and a woman, at that, of bad reputation who has had a procession of lovers, referred to ironically by Jesus as her 'five husbands' (a state of affairs which would automatically have excluded any woman from being recognised by a Rabbi, let alone engaged in conversation). Jesus asks her for a drink of water.

## The Ministry of Jesus

Typical of the beauty and simplicity which so often characterises the earthly image of a great metaphysical truth is this homely request. In the full glare of the noonday sun, He has sat there alone, thirsty and unable to drink. Looking down into the gleaming water of the well, He sees a reflection – of the sun, and of His own face. Then comes this disreputable woman, with a pitcher. It is another substitution. She will give Him a drink; and in return He promises her the Water of Life. This promise and the disconcerting reference to her five 'husbands' are followed by an extraordinary conversation which appears to have nothing to do with what has gone before. The woman suddenly challenges Jesus to defend the attitude of the Jews towards the religious practices of the Samaritans. He tells her:

'The hour cometh when ye shall neither in this mountain nor yet at Jerusalem worship the Father. The hour cometh and *now is* when the true worshippers shall worship the Father in spirit and in truth: for the Father seeketh such to worship him. God is Spirit: and they that worship him must worship in spirit and in truth.'

This extraordinary pronouncement, coming from one who, in outward practice, was an orthodox Jew, has been taken by many people as a licence to give up 'going to church', and an across-the-board justification for a total disregard of 'the letter of the law' in every sphere of human life. It is here that the *time of day* at which the conversation takes place is significant. The sun is at the meridian; 'the hour cometh, and *now is*'. Jesus is speaking directly of the Kingdom of Heaven. In that Kingdom, which is situated at the highest level of Being, where the Spiritual Sun illumines the Void and there is 'no darkness nor shadow cast by turning', there is perfect freedom for the Sons of God.

St Augustine said: 'Love God and do what you like.' But what he *meant* by this all-too-famous remark has seldom been properly understood. Our understanding may be deepened if we pause here for a moment and consider *ourselves*. According to one interpretation of our present-day society, with its tendency to justify the total abandonment of all forms of authority and convention, we are passing into a world age when, *had we been faithful to the direction given us by Jesus*, we should have achieved a state when these freedoms would actually have been permissible and appropriate. In the process of his spiritual journey man has come, so to speak, to that point on the 'line' of his historical time where these freedoms were 'intended' to have been introduced. This then is the 'pattern' of our present: we cannot evade it; and since we are not ready for it we abuse it. Meditation upon this idea will not only elucidate many of the problems immediately facing us; it will help us to *see the paradox* behind the words which Jesus addresses to the woman at the well. Upon this paradox the Mystery of Christianity forever rests. It is the ultimate paradox confronting us in 'this world', where the hour both '*cometh*' and '*now is*'; and that which is best for us is worst, because we make it so by our own choice.

The three synoptic gospels lay tremendous stress upon the miracles performed by Jesus. He Himself did not. One gets the impression that He went to considerable lengths to hush them up. They fall very roughly into two categories: instantaneous healings, and extraordinary interventions into the natural order, including such episodes as the multiplication of the loaves and fishes, the stilling of the wind and waves, walking on the waters of the lake, summoning up the shoal of fish. Within living memory, these 'miracles' were regarded by Christians as a kind of magic unrelated to any system of law on this or any other level of existence. Nowadays this point of view has been abandoned. We know that corresponding wonders have been performed by yogis and shamans, magicians, mystics and saints, at all times and in all parts of the world; and we seek to find the laws by which these things are done, knowing that such laws must exist. There is, however, one aspect of the matter that we tend to forget. Jesus acted from *where He was.*

It is perfectly possible to perform 'miracles', outwardly indistinguishable from those of Jesus, on a level which is accessible to being tested in laboratory experiments. Jesus did not operate from this level because He lived above it. One can operate only from where one is. The miracles of Jesus were supernatural; although one must suppose that the power He was using flowed downwards through all levels, making use of them all in the course of its descent. This does not mean, as our parents and grandparents were disposed to imagine, that He was simply asking favours from God. There is law in Heaven. Jesus was invoking that law, which is unlike our freedom-constricting rules in being itself the definition of freedom. That is one of the many

## The Ministry of Jesus

reasons why His actions were consistently misunderstood. He lived by an absolute law; and His actions, as related in the Gospels, have the flavour of an absolute freedom; He wanders through Judea and Galilee like the breath of the wind, doing as He wills from one moment to the next.

One of the strangest impressions left upon us by the gospel accounts of the Ministry of Jesus is that it was, in a sense, *unimportant* in itself. Its importance seems to lie in something elusive, something which is obvious to us when we see it, but not immediately apparent. The Evangelists present us with a 'scrapbook' of events and sayings, almost as if it scarcely matters what is put in and what is left out. There must have been so much more. But enough is there to demonstrate that Jesus was intentionally building up, by His words and deeds, the necessary *resistance* which would bring about His death. His role requires that He must die. He 'provokes' the world to play its own role, which is that of bringing this about. He derides and mortifies in public the professional theologians and moralists. He overthrows the tables of the shopkeepers. He befriends the prostitute. He provokes by His own luminosity the anger of those whose eyes are blinded by the dust of the world and whose hearts are weighed down by its stones. He calls Judas to be His friend.

They will crucify Him: but of course. . .'*I if I be lifted up from the earth will draw all things\* unto me.*'

---

\*The Authorised Version has 'all men'; but makes it clear that 'men' is an interpolation, not in the original text.

## Chapter Eleven

# *The Vigil of the Passion*

On the eve of His Passion Jesus shares with His disciples the Passover meal.

There is a great deal of conscious deliberation in the way Jesus plans for this occasion; every detail is attended to in advance. Paradoxically, there is a sense of inevitability in every move. The Passover season is chosen by Jesus as the time most appropriate for His sacrificial death; equally it is the predestined time; in going forward deliberately to meet it He is simply affirming that His time *is come*. It stands over against Him. It is here. Nothing can be altered. Yet He plans it all carefully, even down to the 'man bearing a pitcher of water' whom the disciples must follow and who will lead them to the room where the meal is to be prepared. (Many people have seen in this 'water bearer' a symbol of the dawn of the Aquarian age at the expiration of the Piscean, the fish being a recognised symbol of the Christ. This may be so: the Myth is sown with astrological references, to such an extent that one is often tempted to imagine that it is based upon astrology. This is, however, a most misleading assumption: the truth is very far indeed from being so 'obvious'.)

The Pasch or Passover is the ritual commemoration of the delivery of the Jewish people from slavery in Egypt. This story has parallels with that of the deliverance of the Child Jesus and the massacre of the Innocents. In the Old Testament story it is the Lord, not the evil King, who strikes; but in a sense it is always the Lord: everything that happens is a manifestation either of the Wrath or of the Mercy of God. The first-born of the Egyptians are slain to enable the Chosen People to escape. A cry of protest is torn from us as we read of the blood of sacrifice smeared on the doorposts of the Jews – a lamb for each household in substitution

## The Vigil of the Passion

for the first-born child – and the terrible Angel sees the blood and *passes over* that house. Is this, we ask, the God of Love? But we do not understand the meaning of Love nor the way in which we ourselves have chosen to encounter It as Wrath.

The central figure of the Jewish Mystery is the Suffering Servant. In the messianic figure is contained the idea of a sacrificial offering which will at the same time consummate and abolish the blood-sacrifice which has gone before. The Jews in the temple sacrificed lambs, which have always been looked upon as symbolic of innocence. Christians have identified Jesus with the Suffering Servant; and with the *Agnus Dei*, the Lamb of God. The *Agnus Dei* is not, or not only, a mere *symbol* of the Divine Attribute of Innocence. It is the *Sign* in Heaven of that Attribute. A Sufic poem by Jalalu'l-Din Rumi explains the difference:

> 'Twas a fair orchard, full of trees and fruit
> And vines and greenery. A Sufi there
> Sat with eyes closed, his head upon his knee,
> Sunk deep in meditation mystical.
> 'Why', asked another, 'dost thou not behold
> These Signs of God the Merciful displayed
> Around thee, which He bids us contemplate?'
> 'The Signs', he answered, 'I behold within;
> Without is naught but symbols of the Signs.'

The Passover Lamb, too, is not merely a symbol in the Mystery of the Jews. There were *lambs*, yes; as in the Jesus story there were *children* who were slain that He might live. But as there is One Child, there is One Lamb. The Lamb is the Suffering Servant. For Christians, Jesus. (If there is here a seemingly irreconcilable disagreement between the two traditions, this can only be dispelled when both are prepared first to relearn and then to exteriorise the esotericism of their respective Myths.) Jesus, the Jew, identifies Himself explicitly with the Paschal Lamb. At the same time He demonstrates to His disciples, by His action in consecrating the bread and wine as the Signs of His Body and His Blood, that from now on it will no longer be necessary to sacrifice the life of an innocent beast. (As indeed *it never has been necessary*, except from the point of view of those who are in bondage to linear time, and so fail to understand

## The Christian Mystery

that the Sacrifice of the Christ – or the Suffering Servant – has been valid from the Beginning of the World, and has ever been sufficient.) Jesus, at the Last Supper, on the eve of His sacrificial death, takes into His hands the homely fruits of the earth, not in their wild state but as they have been cultivated, harvested and prepared by men to be man's staple food and his life-enhancing drink. These things He declares to be identical with Himself. He has descended (or 'will shortly descend': the tense here is of no significance) into the womb of the earth, that He, being the Principle of Life, may draw all things back, with Him, as He rises to the source of all in God. This is the basis of the Christian Eucharist. It is a revelation of the meaning of sacrifice, and the meaning of food.

Food is the assimilation of one order of being by another. It produces a metamorphosis, as the outcome of a sacrifice, a death.

> I died as mineral and became a plant,
> I died as plant and rose to animal,
> I died as animal and I was Man.
> Why should I fear? When was I less by dying?

That is Rumi, the Sufi. But, beautiful and true as this poem assuredly is, it expresses one side only of the truth. There is a story of the Buddha which relates how, in one of His incarnations, He encounters a starving tigress with her young, and presents Himself to them as food. This story has a meaning similar to that of the Eucharistic rite. It reverses the usual order: instead of the lower being consumed (or eaten) by the higher, in a gesture of Divine generosity the reverse process takes place. The Divine One presents Himself to be eaten. For this, if we accept the idea (which is basic to every tradition) that mankind has become alienated from God, is the necessary condition before man, in the wholeness of his nature, can himself be consumed by the Godhead and so be *made Divine*. If man *in his alienated state* were cast bodily into the Fire of God's Love, that Fire would be for him what the Church has called 'Hell'. He could not endure it for an instant. So God, Who is that Fire, has given us to eat of Himself, so that we may after all become not 'as gods' but as God. That is the meaning of the Eucharist.

Simone Weil, mystic and visionary as she was and herself a

## The Vigil of the Passion

Jew, turned aside from Judaism in disgust, on account of the stress which is laid upon the wrath of God, the necessity of blood-sacrifice, and the punishment of sin. It is true that there is an anthropomorphic element in the Old Testament stories, which makes them, when taken at their face value, undeniably unpleasant; but we should not be misled by what is simply a personification of the Attribute of Wrath. Jesus was not so misled. He knew that the Wrath and the Mercy are reconciled eternally in the One. *Man chooses to encounter the Wrath.* So Jesus prepares for the supreme moment when He will choose with man's choice. He will choose the Wrath, *without having chosen the sin.* In that way the sin itself will pass through Him; and be transmuted into everlasting bliss. For what we know as Wrath is, in God, Love. Jesus will experience It as Wrath; because in the Mystery of His Crucifixion He will surrender Himself wholly to the power of sin. It is said of Him by the Church that He is *made sin* for us. Sinless, He descends into the realm of sin.

The Last Supper represents the gathering together of a number of themes. One of these is the Eucharist. Another is the Mystery of St John. The Beloved Disciple leans upon the bosom of the Lord. He has left his own seat, and is wholly united with Jesus at this moment – an identification to be re-emphasised later on, when Jesus speaks to His Mother and to this disciple from the Cross, telling them that they are now to regard themselves as mother and son: *and from that hour the disciple took her unto his own.* This passage has generally been interpreted as meaning that Jesus, being about to die, was asking John to look after Mary in a practical sense. But Jesus had not been looking after His mother in that sense for years. On the contrary, He had been wandering about the countryside as an itinerant preacher, earning no money and renouncing the normal obligations of family life. The passage in question seems more like an allusion, in the veiled language typical of the fourth gospel, to the mysterious vocation of John as the future representative of the Divine Principle at present incarnate in the dying Jesus. John, having lain upon the heart of his Lord, undergoes a metamorphosis. Centuries later, another St John (of the Cross) was to write of this mystical transformation in poetry so erotic and strange that cautious churchmen of his time raised their eyebrows in astonishment.

## The Christian Mystery

> Lost to myself I strayed,
> My face upon my lover having laid . . .
>
> Oh night that joined the lover
> To the beloved bride
> Transfiguring them each into the other . . .

The 'beloved bride' here is the soul of the mystic. One interpretation of the figure of St John is that he represents the soul in mystical union with the Christ. The idea that he is, or will be, in some sense himself the Christ, refers to a future Great Cycle of time. There is a tradition to this effect. A number of the post-Christian Mystery Schools, outside the official boundaries of the Church, refer to it.

Another theme which appears in the gospel accounts of the Last Supper is that of the Departure of Judas. The Eucharistic meal is the occasion of what is perhaps the most baffling and terrible episode in the whole of the New Testament – the confirmation by Jesus of the role of the Betrayer, His giving of the sop to Judas, as if it were the very sacrament of death. 'And after the sop Satan entered into him. Then said Jesus unto him, That thou doest do quickly . . . He then having received the sop went immediately out: and it was night.' Jesus has spoken in the present tense: 'that thou doest'. Judas has chosen, is choosing, and will forever choose, in all eternity, to reject the Christ. In ratifying that choice, Jesus is pronouncing the edict of man's freedom, without which the Cosmic Drama of God's Love could never be played out. He actually commands Judas: 'That thou doest, *do*.'

The Myth is concerned with the ultimate possibilities which are open to mankind. It is necessary that all these possibilities should be represented in it, because all these possibilities are eternally existent. In eternity they *are*. Total annihilation is one of them. The terrible concept of an Everlasting Hell is a way of expressing the idea that the Void is filled, ultimately, with the Love of God: therefore to choose the Void is to choose to be consumed by that Fire without being in any way responsive to It, as an alien substance forever rejecting the Divine. Judas, in the Myth, is the type of this Rejection. His is the role of the Betrayer, the one who, having been chosen by God and knowing the

## The Vigil of the Passion

Saviour face to face, knowing therefore precisely what he does, deliberately chooses to betray Him – and, having so chosen, gives way to despair and casts himself into the outer darkness in an orgasm of remorse. Judas hangs himself; and, according to one apocryphal tradition not to be found in the canonical New Testament, as he does so his entrails burst asunder – a horrible image of disintegration unchecked.

Christians have never been encouraged to speculate about the *historical* Judas. To do so is almost inevitably to fall into one of two errors: either we mentally consign a fellow human-being to Hell or we cannot bear to do this, and refuse altogether to see the meaning and necessity of his role in the Myth. The Judas of history is the greatest enigma of the New Testament. We do not know, have no means of knowing, and *do not need to know* to what extent he corresponded to the Mythical Judas. The latter is the ultimate paradox. He represents Man in a state of non-existence. He is totally inhuman because he has intentionally rejected the Divine Humanity of the Christ. The Christian Mystery demands that we should *love one another in Christ*, this being the definition of human love. Therefore we cannot love Judas as we encounter him in the Myth. If we find this unbearable, we may seek consolation (and there is always consolation if we know how to find it: the Mystery of our being is the Mystery of Love) in a hidden teaching, seldom mentioned because it is so hard to understand and so easy to misinterpret. This tells us that the role of Judas in the Eternal Drama of the Passion which is forever being played out (whether or not it was ever completely enacted on our own particular line of historical time), because it belongs by definition to a 'non-being' who does not exist, is assumed under obedience by one of God's servants. It was this esoteric teaching which prompted the contemporary sage and mystic J. G. Bennet actually to declare that Judas was himself the sacrificial victim who was 'made sin' for our sake.

The other disciples are types of us all. They will fail (as He warns them); and then again, as a new cycle comes round, they will triumph in Him. They have chosen Him (or have been chosen by Him) in Eternity, and that choice will eventually 'make them whole': a connection never ceases to exist between each individual soul and its first and last and essential act of choice. So there is able to be a brief period of intimate

## The Christian Mystery

communion between the Lord and His chosen disciples on the eve of His death. In the Gospel of St John He speaks to them and prays aloud in their presence, in words which contain some of the greatest metaphysical statements in the scriptures of the world: 'I am the Way, the Truth and the Life: no man cometh unto the Father but by me . . . And I will give you another Comforter, that he may abide with you for ever; the Spirit of truth whom the world cannot receive because it seeth him not, neither knoweth him: but ye know him . . . because I live ye shall live also . . .'

The last discourse of the Lord, sublime as it is, is easy to misinterpret. He speaks to these beloved disciples as if they were a tiny band of chosen ones taken out of 'the world'; so that, reading superficially, without having realised the timeless metaphysical character of what is being said, we could be (and a great many people have been) led to suppose that only a very few, highly favoured individuals will eventually be included in what is here referred to as 'my Father's house'. This is totally to misunderstand the level of the Lord's discourse. 'The world', in the Gospel of St John, is that which is not the Christ. The disciples are ourselves. In that tiny band are the types of all men everywhere who in eternity have chosen God, not of their own virtue but because they have been chosen by Him, having first been re-called by Jesus to partake of His Eucharist as members of His Mystical Church. (To ask, as we tend to do, whether or not this promise of salvation covers the totality of mankind, is simply to pose an unanswerable question. It seems possible, however, that to choose God rather than Hell – and there is no other choice – is the very definition and condition of existence, here or anywhere else.) When Jesus, addressing the Father, says 'They are not of the world, even as I am not of the world', He means that in so far as we adhere to Him we belong not to the realm of 'gravity' but to that of 'grace'.

Neither is there any question here of denigrating the partial beauties and realities of our experienced world. Jesus is not likely to be speaking of His Father's creation as if it were to be summarily dismissed. (His constant references elsewhere to the beauty and goodness of the natural world, together with His habitual participation in everyday human enjoyments, should put this beyond dispute.) Three meanings of the word 'world' require to be distinguished at this point: (1) the meaning as

## The Vigil of the Passion

intended here by St John; (2) the meaning which refers to our own precarious divided *state*; and (3) the notion popular today of a sentimental 'holy' world which is spoken of as if it were here and now in existence. The third of these 'meanings' is not a meaning at all; it is a nonsense. Our world is not a *place*; it is a *state*. It is not in itself 'holy'; it is not perfectible; it is not even, except here and there, for a short time, improvable by our efforts. The balance of it is held in a constant polarity between the evil and the good. *The Christian Mystery has to do with states.* Seven of these are easily distinguishable and can be named: Heaven (the Presence of God); Paradise (the state of innocence); 'this world', as St John uses the term; 'this world' as we commonly experience it; Purgatory; Limbo; and Hell. These distinctions will gradually become clearer as we go on. Meanwhile it is necessary to understand that *all* these states are present in our own; and that each state is *a mode of experiencing the totality of them all*. This totality is, and can only be, God. The state one is in depends entirely upon oneself.

In the apocryphal scripture known as the Acts of John, the place of the Last Discourse is taken by a round dance accompanied by a kind of litany or hymn. This hymn is, in its own strange way, as beautiful as anything in the canonical Gospels. It is a continuous play upon paradox – 'I would be saved and I would save . . . I would be wounded and I would wound . . . I would be eaten and I would eat', and so on, as the disciples dance in a ring around the Lord. 'Grace danceth. I would pipe. Dance ye all. I would lament. Lament ye all.' And finally, at the conclusion of the hymn: 'A mirror am I to thee that beholdest me. A door am I to thee that knockest at me. A way am I to thee a wayfarer.'

It seems fairly clear that the canonical Last Discourse and this extraordinary hymn do not come from the same hand, although they have much in common and both are associated with St John. In both cases we are given to understand that the Lord was preparing His disciples for what was to come by initiating them into some of the innermost secrets of His role upon earth. The Acts of John tell us that He afterwards exhorted them not to speak of what they had seen and heard. The canonical Gospel brings the Last Discourse to an end with the awe-inspiring cry: 'O righteous Father, the world hath not known thee, but I have known thee, and these have known thee that thou hast sent me. And I have declared unto them thy name and will declare it, that the love wherewith thou hast loved me may be in them and I in them.'

After this, we are told, 'He went forth with His disciples over the brook Cedron, where was a garden.'

Gardens figure constantly in the world of myth. More often than not, they are places of false allurements. The 'kindly fruits of the earth', from the apple of Eden to the wares of Goblin market, have always had an evil aspect (like everything else), appearing as seductive emissaries from the world below, luring men downwards by the magic of identification by the tasting of food (as in the story of Persephone and the Hadean pomegranate) to the place of their own twisting roots. The grape, most seductive of them all, was set apart by Jesus as the symbol of His own blood, a sign of the redemption of the world; so that, drinking its juice, men might be raised up into communion with Him. In this act He redeemed the entirety of the fallen fruits of the Paradise garden. 'God Almighty', wrote Francis Bacon, 'first planted a garden.' And God Almighty is redeeming this wasted earth by re-planting it in Heaven as a New Garden; so that we, as we participate in that process, making our own little gardens here and now, may continually rejoice.

Jesus chose to appear in His Risen Body to the woman who loved Him in a garden. Although we are not told what trees and flowers were growing there, the logic of the Myth would seem to indicate a burgeoning of springtime blossom, soft colours, vernal freshness, morning light. The garden of Gethsemane was very different.

The place where Jesus chooses to suffer the agony of His moment of choice, that supreme moment when He enters into the meaning of His own Act and chooses it with the entirety of Himself, is a garden of olives, the fruit above all others which embodies the *kindness* of nature in relation to men. Olives are dusky green and smooth. They represent the oil used for the anointing of kings and priests and those about to die. Pure oil is traditionally a sacred substance. It contains fire; and yet it has a healing touch, as if it were nature's communication of the Tenderness of God. Jesus enters into the olive grove alone. It is dark. His disciples have gone to sleep.

## The Vigil of the Passion

The moment of the acceptance by Jesus of His role and the moment of the acceptance by the Virgin of Hers are one and the same. They exist upon a single point, making each other possible, each in each. Out of the union of these two Acts issues the redemption of the world. 'Behold the handmaid of the Lord. Be it unto me according to thy word.' The scene is cool and passionless, as the totally purified, spiritualised creature surrenders in serenity and simplicity to the Voice which is neither a plea nor yet a command but simply the opening up of a possibility for the world and for Herself. Mary chooses to accept. But before She can do so there has to be that other choice, that other acceptance, which only God-in-Man is strong enough to make. Jesus has to enter wholly into the realm of death. The moment of His choice involves every level of His being in anguish. Even His body sweats blood. He says:

'O my Father, if it be possible let this cup pass from me: nevertheless not as I will but as thou wilt.'

One could spend a lifetime meditating on the distinction implicit in these words between the 'I' of Jesus as He prays and That in Him which is wholly in union with the Will of God. He does not say '*I* will' but 'Be it not as *I* will. Be it as Thou wilt.' He does not pretend that *he* wills it. The little ego cannot will to be extinguished in agony. This would be a contradiction in terms. The little ego is the very principle in us which says 'I'.

Again it is neither a command nor a plea to which the Lord responds. It is the movement of Love whereby God offers the world to Himself. In Christ He accepts His own gift. It is the gift of a stone. Deep in the heart of gravity, body, soul and spirit must be crushed until there is nothing left.

'Could ye not watch with me one hour?' Jesus asks His disciples when He finds them asleep. 'Watch and pray,' He exhorts them, as He Himself prepares for the ordeal of the night, in the course of which He will be led before one after another of His judges, subjected in the intervals to physical and mental maltreatment, deserted by His disciples, howled at by the mob. '*Wake* and pray' is an alternative, and probably more accurate, translation. Our world is in the state of being half asleep while all around us the Son of Man is being spat upon and done to death.

The ordeal of the night before the Passion begins in an awesome and dreadful manner with a kiss. The kiss of Judas is the reverse image of the Mystical Kiss which has always been the sign of union between the soul and Christ. It ends with them leading Him away, in the cold light of dawn, to the hill which is called Golgotha, meaning the place of a skull. In Christian art the Crucifixion is frequently depicted as being enacted above the burial place of Adam's skull, as if that skull were the root from which springs the Tree of the Cross. It is not until high noon that they raise Him up. We see that this cannot be otherwise. God must encounter death in the full glare of publicity, naked in the face of the sun; just as He becomes incarnate in the world, secretly, in the dark. (God does not die and is not born: Jesus is born and dies; God, in Jesus, comes into the world and there *encounters* death.) It is only by a kind of heavenly courtesy on the part of the creatures that the sun and moon conceal their faces in the final moment and darkness covers the face of the earth.

## Chapter Twleve

# *The Cross*

We are approaching the supreme moment of the Christian Mystery: the Passion of the Christ.

The Crucifixion and the Resurrection of the Lord are the opposite aspects of His primary Act in creating the heavens and the earth. They are eternally united, as what the Chinese call the Yin and the Yang. Most of us are familiar with this idea as depicted in the form of a globe divided equally into dark and light, with a point of darkness in the light and of light in the dark. *In time* it is the darkness which 'comes first'. The Void must be empty 'before' it can be filled. That is the way we time-bound creatures see it; not the way it *is*. In Eternity the Triumph of the Resurrection is *prior* to the Agony and the Death. Without the Resurrection no-thing would be (this is literally true: in so far as no-thing can *be*, there would *be* no-thing, and no-thing else; since that is what the Crucifixion essentially is, a contradiction in terms, an unthinkable thought). The Crucifixion *by itself* could not possibly have taken place in time as a physical event. It is the very image of non-existence. (Incidentally, the idea that the Events of the Myth take place – as they must – 'in time' does not of necessity imply the *historicity* of the entire story as it stands. Our illusions about time are such that we can only very hazily imagine what this mysterious phenomenon really is, not as we experience it, but in itself as a necessary mode of the Providence of God.)

Jesus dies; and in Him the Godhead *encounters* death. This Event represents not only a Metaphysical Reality but the innermost essence of our personal and communal experience. It shows us *what is happening to us* – not as it appears to us to be, but *as it is*. The Crucified and Resurrected Christ is not a remote figure involved in some incomprehensible Mystery unrelated to the world we know: He is the one and only *explanation* of the world we know. Golgotha is the cancer ward, the concentration camp, the Calcutta street where the dying lie in the dust and filth. Golgotha is the heart of the mother who gives birth to a malformed or mentally retarded child. Until we can see this, really see it, we shall not understand what the story of the Passion is about.

There are as many ways of approaching this central Mystery of Christianity as there are points upon the surface of a globe. Every aspect of theology, every episode of the Myth, every utterance of the saints, if pursued a little way will be found to lead directly back to it. And not only that. There is not a single created thing, not a human being alive or dead, not a happening past or present, which is not potentially capable of doing the same. We may start where we choose. All ways eventually lead us to the parting of the ways, which is the Cross. If we are choosing here to initiate a meditation upon the sexual imagery associated with the Passion, this is partly because the very unusualness of the exercise will give our minds a jolt. (It is not exceptional for spiritual teachers and Esoteric Schools to recommend a certain kind of 'shock treatment'.) References to the intimate connection between sexuality and the Crucifixion of Jesus are ubiquitous in the literature of Christianity, but deliberately oblique. The cosmic significance of the sexual act is an image – and more than an 'image' – of the Passion of Christ. It is intimately and essentially fused with the Moment of the Cross. The moment of Life is the moment of Death, occurring on what T. S. Eliot calls 'the point of intersection of the timeless with time'. It is on account of the absolute paradoxicality of this primal moment that the act of generation has had, from the point of view of Christianity, a double face. The orgasm of ecstasy is, in a blinding mystery which has almost never been exposed because the Church has considered it to be at once too holy and too terrible to contemplate, the cry of dereliction from the Cross. The words which follow that cry are plainer in the Latin even than in the English text: It is finished – *Consummatum est.*

To understand this we must look more deeply than we have already done into some of the ideas which lie behind the universal human instinct to offer sacrifice to the gods. Sacrifice is the

## The Cross

intentional creation of a *void to be filled*. At the heart of all the great traditions is a dark mystery, seldom explained but constantly determining the pattern of the rites. We may call this the law of *displacement*. It means that wherever there is a joy there will be a corresponding pain; wherever there is union, division; wherever there is the orgasm of coming-to-be there will also be the spasm of death. All things are held in an eternal balance. So that if, to assist our understanding, we think of a figure which is half light and half dark (the Yin-Yang is an obvious and aesthetically beautiful example, with its curving lines suggesting the multidimensionality of the cosmic 'globe') then we may proceed to the idea that every point of light which passes over into the darkness, every point of darkness which passes over into the light, will displace a corresponding point, in order to find room for itself; and so in a constant to-ing and fro-ing the balance will be sustained, unless and until a time comes when it suddenly, instantaneously, tips – the darkness becomes light, the entire figure is transformed into the sun; whereupon there proceeds from it once more its eternal twin, and the cosmic process commences once again. The image is of course preposterously inadequate; but it serves to introduce the idea that in *asking* for something we must always be prepared, in some way, to *give* its equivalent; that by suffering we may bring about joy; and by grasping at bliss we must, by an inexorable law, be responsible for pain. This is the underlying theme of many of the old games which are played by children, games which, before they were simply that and nothing more, were ancient rites with origins going back to the time when men first began consciously to participate in the cosmic dance – 'Nuts in May', for instance ('who will you *send* to fetch her away?').

A ritual sacrifice is an offering intended to effect a *displacement*. The rites of black magic are based upon the same idea: to bring about evil one intentionally sets up an orgy of sexual indulgence. And here it is vital to understand that neither of these rituals actually *works* in the sense which has been popularly supposed; neither has there ever been an enlightened seer who has taught that they do. The truth which underlies them is of a grandeur infinitely exceeding the small-minded notion that we can actually induce the gods, let alone the One

## The Christian Mystery

God, to give us some specific thing because we have 'sacrificed' something else. There are two senses only in which such rituals can be said to 'work'. The first is by suggestion. The exercise of mental power can bring about almost any effect in proportion to its strength. The performance of an appropriate ritual assists this process. The more impressive and even painful the ritual the more effectual it is likely to be in providing this assistance. However, this is not the most profound justification for the performance of a rite, whether this be a symbolic sacrifice or a love-feast or a dance or any other formal re-enactment of the Cosmic Event. The real justification of ritual resides in the spiritual and physical involvement of the participants in what Simone Weil called 'the Order of the World'. A sincerely performed ritual coinheres in that Order. It is not a demand made of God; but the conscious adoption of a role. We have to accept and affirm and learn, and if possible ritualise, and at all times *play the parts* allotted to us in the sacrificial Drama of the Death and Resurrection of the Christ.

Christians have frequently made the claim that *before* the Crucifixion the blood-sacrifice of animals was legitimate, although inadequate; while *after* that event (considered of course as an episode in linear time) the Old Law was superseded and its practices made obsolete. This is the old mistake. The historic biography of Jesus should never be thought of as cutting through linear time and slicing it in two, so that what was not true BC is true AD: this is to mistake both the nature of time and the nature of historic events. The historic event of the Crucifixion was the near-perfect re-enactment in a concentrated span of time and space of the Crucifixion of the God-Man which *is* at the Foundation of the world. This Crucifixion is the one and only sacrifice, eternally complete. All that we need to do is to identify ourselves with it, suffering *in* it, dying *in* it, and this we do essentially by a turning of the will. The rites are but means to that end. They affirm our intention and draw us together in an outward and visible pattern which mirrors upon earth the Divine Order of the Kingdom of God.

The Dark and the Light are the twin polarities of the One. Love and Death, the Plenitude and the Void, continuously play with one another, dancing together like those medieval angels on the needle's point. In the Hindu tradition, as may be seen from

## The Cross

the images which smother the exterior walls of many temples in South India, this playing, dancing, or coupling is symbolised by the act of sex, which thus becomes the primary symbol, as for Christians the primary symbol is the Cross. Christianity, however, does possess an overt sexual image, albeit one which is never visually reproduced, in the Heavenly Nuptials of the Virgin which are celebrated at the End of the World, on the 'other side' of death. In those Nuptials, which are also referred to as the Mystical Union between Christ and His Church, all Christian marriages are said to coinhere; a point which is explicitly stressed in the marriage service, and which explains why the sexual act within marriage is regarded as a sacrament. The Nuptials of the Virgin are associated with what mystics all down the ages have described as the Divine Kiss, which constitutes the Union between the soul and Christ. The Cross is the 'shadow side' of this Mystery of the Kiss. In the Myth it is the Dark Bride of the Crucified God. He who hangs upon it is the same Who creates the worlds by an Act of Love.

The idea of the Cross as Bride is confirmed by innumerable litanies, prayers and hymns, extolling it in words very similar to those which are used of the Virgin Herself. One would naturally suppose that Christians would denounce the instrument of Christ's death. But this is far from being the case. On Good Friday there is a liturgical service known as the Adoration of the Cross. Relics of the True Cross abounded throughout Christendom, until the tradition grew up that every church must possess such a relic, and no high altar could be dedicated until this infinitely precious and life-bestowing object had been placed within it. St Anselm, in a well-known prayer, apostrophises the Cross as ecstatically as if he were addressing the Mother of God: 'Dear Cross . . . precious wood . . . worshipful sign . . . Cruel men prepared thee for the gentle lamb but their stupid blasphemy enters not into our thought of thee; rather we see thee in the light of that wisdom and love which made Him accept thee . . . By thee the world is made new and adorned with the light of truth . . . by thee the holy celestial city is rebuilt . . . In thee and by thee is my salvation and my life.' It is a very long prayer, typical of many recited by the Church. Perhaps the most beautiful of them all is the *Pange Lingua*, the great Good Friday Hymn with the solemn refrain:

## The Christian Mystery

> Faithful Cross, of trees created,
> Noblest tree of all art thou.
> Forest none bears trees as thou art,
> Like in leaf or flower or bough . . .

Noblest tree . . . Here we have a link with the Tree of Life, the World Tree of a thousand names, Ygg drasil ('best of all trees'), from which Odin hung nine days and nights to read the runes that are written in space.

> I know that I hung
> On the windswept tree
> For nine full nights
> Wounded with a spear,
> Given to Odin,
> Myself to myself
> On that tree
> Of which men know not
> From what roots it rises.
>
> They did not comfort me with bread
> Or with the drinking horn.
> I peered downward,
> I grasped the runes,
> Screeching I grasped them.

The World Tree is the Cosmic Axis linking the many levels of being: the Tree of the Sephiroth, Jacob's ladder, Jack's beanstalk. Sometimes, as in the case of the Maypole, it seems like a phallic symbol, unmistakably male. In Christian terms, however, it is the female aspect of a twofold figure of which the male aspect is the Christ. The Crucifix is a symbol corresponding to the Tantric images of coupling gods. The difference is that it expresses anguish rather than bliss. The seed of life which is spilled on the Cross is carried in a stream of blood.

The Christ-figure on the Crucifix represents both the Heavenly Bridegroom Himself, and the Divine Phallus upraised in the Creative Act:

*I if I be lifted up shall draw all men unto Me.*

Christians have frequently been shocked by the overt manner in which Hindus worship the Phallus of Shiva, the Creator God.

## The Cross

They have never interpreted the symbolism under which they themselves do precisely that. Jesus is uplifted on the Cross. Traditional iconography depicts this uplifting as the first stage of the awesome drama, an echo of which is found in the Church's calendar as the Feast of the Exaltation of the Cross, overtly a celebration of its rediscovery and subsequent setting up as an object of adoration by the Christian world. In painting after painting we see the dreadful instrument of the Passion rearing up at an angle from the ground with the passive figure pinioned helplessly against it, unable to resist. This is, amongst other things, a gruesomely painful image of the prelude to the sexual act. The entire drama of the Passion is a veiled and darkly sombre presentation of this act, which is here identified with the total dereliction and ultimate solitude of death. *In my End is my Beginning* – but nothing remains to remind us of this hope. The meaning of the scene would be lost if a hint of the resurrection were contained in it.

In medieval churches, by a firmly established custom, the group consisting of the Crucified Christ with the Virgin and St John was represented on a beam above the sanctuary entrance. The Woman and the Man face one another, divided by the Cross. In numerous paintings and carvings of the same scene the motif is repeated in the sun and the moon, who look on from above, their faces veiled, their lights put out. The group is representative of the Mystery of sexuality *as that which crucifies the Christ*. The ecstasy coinheres in the agony. The all but incomprehensible ambiguity of the Christian attitude towards sex is implicit in this scene. Often it contains another figure – the Magdalen who represents the Virgin's 'other self'. She kneels in the central position at the foot of the Cross, her flaming unbound hair the symbol alike of her abundant sexuality and of its fiery sacrifice. Here the sexuality which is potential in the Virgin, actualised in the Prostitute, is surrendered to the Love of God. The wholeness of the Virgin will be actualised, the promiscuity of the Prostitute will be gathered together into a single Act of ecstatic acceptance ('Be it unto me according to thy word') when the two Marys are eternally united as the Bride of Christ.

Meanwhile there is the 'reverse aspect' of that ultimate bliss. We are looking at Heaven now *from the point of view of sin*. Jesus hangs suspended for three hours upon the Cross 'and there was a

## The Christian Mystery

darkness over all the earth'. At the end of that time we are told that He 'cried with a loud voice'. This is the dreadful cry of dereliction, the orgasm of death. 'And behold the veil of the temple was rent from the top to the bottom; and the earth did quake . . .' The veil of the temple protected the sanctuary known as the Holy of Holies which could only be entered by the High Priest. It corresponds to the hymen protecting the virginal womb. (The Blessed Virgin has frequently been identified with *Shekinah*, the awesome Mystery of Divine Femininity Whose Presence filled the Holy of Holies, as She hovered above and around the Ark of the Covenant.)

St John's Gospel does not speak of a cry. Instead we are told that Jesus, 'knowing that all things were now accomplished', said 'It is finished' and, bowing His head, 'gave up the ghost'. The four accounts of these last moments are not entirely consistent with each other, but in all of them there is this final orgasm of anguish followed by the relief of death. Afterwards 'one of the soldiers with a spear pierced his side and there came out blood and water'. This is the fifth of the traditional 'five wounds'. The five wounds correspond to (amongst innumerable other things) the five senses: we are meant to understand that every one of the sensual pleasures of fallen man becomes a wound in the side of Christ. It is a hard saying; but only in the ultimate Heaven and the Garden of Innocence does it cease to be true. Both of these states are present with us in this world; but neither one of them is wholly present. Therein is the ambiguity and the paradox from which we are unable to escape this side of death.

There are many traditional representations of the Deposition. In all these paintings the body of the Lord is shown as collapsing limply into the arms of the waiting disciples, in total contrast to its appearance in the first stage of the drama, when the Cross is being erected and the body stretched out upon it is taut and hard. Again the sexual symbolism is apparent. The Mother of Jesus receives Him in Her arms. This is the *pietà* scene, presented for the veneration of the people in every Catholic church. The Divine Organ of Generation lies across a woman's lap. In Michelangelo's *Pietà* the woman is no more than a girl; and, historically impossible as this may be, we feel it to be right. This is the Eternal Mary: the two Marys, mother and lover, watching over the sleep of the Beloved.

## The Cross

After one has read the gospel accounts of the Crucifixion, it is difficult to find anything else written on the subject which seems even remotely worthy of it. One poem stands out, consummate in its beauty and majesty, Anglo-Saxon, of the seventh century, appropriately anonymous. It is known as 'The Dream of the Rood'.

>A dream came to me
>   at deep midnight
>when humankind
>   kept their beds
>– the dream of dreams
>   I shall declare it.
>
>It seemed I saw the Tree itself
>borne on the air, light wound about it,
>– a beam of brightest wood, a beacon clad
>in overlapping gold, glancing gems
>fair at its foot, and five stones
>set in a crux flashed from the crosstree.
>
>Around angels of God
>   All gazed upon it
>since first fashioning fair.
>   It was not a felon's gallows,
>for holy ghosts beheld it there,
>and men on mould, and the whole Making shone for it
>– signum of victory.
>               Stained and marred,
>stricken with shame, I saw the glory-tree
>shine out gaily, sheathed in yellow
>decorous gold; and gemstones made
>for their Maker's Tree a right mail-coat.
>
>Yet through the masking gold I might perceive
>what terrible sufferings were once sustained thereon:
>it bled from the right side.
>   Ruth filled my heart.
>
>Affrayed I saw that unstill brightness
>change raiment and colour
>– again clad in gold
>or again slicked with sweat,
>   spangled with spilling blood.

## The Christian Mystery

Yet lying there a long while
I beheld, sorrowing, the Healer's Tree
till it seemed that I heard how it broke silence,
best of wood, and began to speak:

'Over that long remove my mind ranges
back to the holt where I was hewn down;
from my own stem I was struck away;
   dragged off by strong enemies,
wrought into a roadside scaffold.
   They made me a hoist for wrongdoers.

The soldiers on their shoulders bore me,
   until on a hill-top they set me up;
many enemies made me fast there.
   Then I saw, marching towards me,
mankind's brave King.
   He came to climb upon me.

I dared not break or bend aside
against God's will, though the ground itself
shook at my feet. Fast I stood,
who falling could have felled them all.

Almighty God ungirded Him,
   eager to mount the gallows,
unafraid in the sight of many:
   He would set free mankind.
I shook when His arms embraced me
   but I durst not bow to ground,
stoop to earth's surface.
   Stand fast I must.

I was reared up, a rood.
   I raised the great King,
liege lord of the heavens,
   dared not lean from the true.
They drove me through with dark nails:
   on me are the deep wounds manifest,
Wide-mouthed hate-dents.
   I durst not harm any of them.
How they mocked at us both!
   I was all moist with blood
Sprung from the Man's side
   after He sent forth His soul.

## The Cross

Wry wierds a many I underwent
up on that hill-top; saw the Lord of Hosts
stretched out stark. Darkness shrouded
the King's corse. Clouds wrapped
its clean shining. A shade went out
wan under cloud-pall. All creation wept,
keened the King's death. Christ was on the Cross.

But there quickly came from far
earls to the One there. All that I beheld;
had grown weak with grief,
    Yet with glad will bent then
meek to those men's hands,
    yielded Almighty God.

They lifted Him down from the leaden pain,
    left me, the commanders,
standing in a sweat of blood.
    I was all wounded with shafts.

They straightened out His strained limbs,
    stood at His body's head,
looked down on the Lord of Heaven
    – for a while. He lay there resting –
set to contrive Him a tomb
    in the sight of the Tree of Death,
carved it of bright stone,
    laid in it the Bringer of victory,
spent from the great struggle.
    They began to speak the grief-song,
said in the sinking light,
    they thought to set out homeward;
their hearts were sick to death,
    their most high Prince
they left to rest there with scant retinue.

Yet we three, weeping a good while
stood in that place after the song had gone up
from the captains' throats. Cold grew the corse,
fair soul-house.

              They felled us all.
We crashed to ground, cruel Wierd,
and they delved for us a deep pit.

*The Christian Mystery*

The Lord's men learnt of it,
His friends found me . . .
It was they who girt me with gold and silver . . .'

## Chapter Thirteen

# *The Risen Body*

The Act of Oblation is accomplished. Now Christ the Seed is buried in the tomb or womb, to emerge as the risen Lord, the Living God.

The tomb in which they lay Him is the same from which He originally came forth. This is implied in the mythical identity of the two Josephs. Joseph of Arimathea offers the 'new tomb' which he has had prepared for himself. This cave or tomb is in a fair garden. It is the womb of the Virgin. Joseph, we are told, has *bought* the garden: legally it is his property. In the same way Mary was the wife of the other Joseph according to the law. He had a husband's rights over her body, to implant his seed in it. But like the second Joseph he relinquished those rights. So we are given to understand that the Descent of the Divine Being into matter is itself an entombment: the Annunciation to Mary and the laying of His body in the cave are two modes of the same Event. He *falls* with the fall of man. The garden is the world; its cave is the point at which He enters the world and from which He departs from it and at which He returns. It opens into the void at creation's root from which space and time emerge and into which they must eventually flow back. The physical situation of this point is the centre of the earth. Seed-like, the Lord descends. But this descent is so deep that no earthly seed could endure it and live. Nothing could survive in this region without being completely sucked down, were it not for the saving action of the Christ, Who forever descends and ascends with the souls He has released. Without Christ, the world would be irretrievably sucked back into itself.

According to the words of the Creed, 'He descended into Hell'. Christians have attempted to modify this statement by suggesting that it refers to Limbo, the realm of waiting, where the patriarchs and prophets of the Old Testament awaited their deliverance by Jesus. The Descent into Limbo is generally depicted as the arrival of Jesus at the mouth of a pit, to be greeted by Adam and his descendants. This is one of the great moments of the Myth. But the Creed still uses the word 'Hell'.

The Lord visits Limbo at some point during the three days between His entombment and His rising from the dead. Limbo is a kind of *ante-room* of Hell; in fact the issue has been greatly confused by a tendency among writers, following Dante, to use an image of concentric circles in describing Hell; so that Limbo is presented as the first circle, the place of disconsolate ghosts. The Church, forgetting its own esotericism, became needlessly embarrassed by the question of what happens to unbaptised babies and the 'good pagans' who have never heard of the Christian Faith. It consigned them to Limbo – more or less for ever, with the reservation that they might perhaps be released at the Day of Judgement. Thus Limbo, from being a waiting-room for the saints of the Old Dispensation, became a kind of Hell without the everlasting torments. All this, however, is an exoteric confusion. The real Limbo is familiar to us all. It corresponds to the state of somnambulance, of falling asleep. It is subject to gravity: we *sink into it*. In this state our responsibility is diminished. As Gurdjieff was constantly explaining, we cannot *do*. We spend the greater part of our so-called 'waking' lives in this state; and by doing so make ourselves impotent.

One meaning behind the concept of Limbo is similar to that of Julian's parable of the servant. The servant was not condemned, because he did not *choose* to fall; he fell when he was not in touch with the innermost essence of himself. So he found himself lying in his ditch by a kind of accident. The ditch is the realm of 'gravity' as opposed to that of 'grace'. Limbo is more nearly a 'process' than any other single moment of the Myth: that is why it can be represented simply as a state of sleepiness or as the state of being absolutely hemmed in by impenetrable rock. It is the state of *falling into* the bondage of time, a spiralling vortex into the centre of the earth. Christ, in the three days of His Cosmic Descent, enters this vortex and travels down it to its nethermost point. On His way, He releases those souls who are trapped in it and *desire to be released*. The Old Testament saints are types of these souls, that is to say of us all, in the sense that, like Paul, we

## The Risen Body

protest that the evil we would not, we do – and, like Paul, we cry out in our hearts to the Lord: 'Who will deliver me from this death?'

Jesus releases the 'servant'. But then He travels on. He sinks through the uttermost reaches of gravity until, at the centre of the worlds, He comes upon the nethermost point. This nethermost point is the Fire of God's Love. It is Heaven and Hell. For the God-hater, Hell; for the mystic, the Heaven within. The apex and the centre are one. It is from this point, the point of the Burning Fire at the heart of the implacable stone, that He rises from the dead.

Easter is the Festival of Light. It is wholly different from Christmas in that now the Light is total, All-Triumphant – all the levels of being, body, soul and spirit, are transfigured by it. *Now* is the metamorphosis of this world into the Kingdom of God, of Man into the glorified Body of the Christ. If we think of Christmas as a tiny point of Light appearing, and gradually increasing, in a world of darkness, Easter is the infinite expansion of that point into a sphere of Heavenly Radiance. So the Church cries, in greeting, on Easter morning: *Lumen Christi! Deo Gratias!* The Paschal candle is lit in anticipation of the rising sun. That sun, our physical orb, is our 'candle', dimmed in its rising by a greater Sun, before Whose Brightness it is less than the tiniest flame we can kindle here on earth. Hermes Trismegistus, writing of that Other Sun, speaks of It as 'set up in the midst and wearing the cosmos as a wreath'. This is a direct reference to the representations of the Solar Apollo in the Mysteries of ancient Rome. For the Crucified Christ, the cosmos is a wreath of thorns. But in His Resurrection the awful spikes turn gold and become the rays of the glory of God.

The cave from which the Risen Lord comes forth is the same from which Theseus, having battled with the Minotaur in the underground labyrinth, emerges triumphant. The story of Theseus provides a bridge-image linking the resurrection myths with those of the slaying of dragons, of which the most familiar to us is that of St George. The rescued princess is a type of the human soul. In Mystery plays and rituals from all over the world, the moment of deliverance is celebrated by a rapturous dance. A sixteenth-century Dutch poet, Joost van der Vondel, puts into the mouth of Adam the meaning of it all:

## The Christian Mystery

> Learn to dance the festive measure
>     Which the Lord
> God invented in his leisure;
> Imitate with knowing pleasure
>     Heaven's chord.
>
> If you'd change to forms supernal
>     Fields of earth,
> Follow heaven's course diurnal:
> Stars obey the role eternal
>     Of their birth . . .

Changing to 'forms supernal' is the point of Easter and the point of the dance. Ritual dancing is the re-enactment in time of the Order which exists in Heaven. That Order is movement around a central stillness. Easter Day is Dancing Day. An anonymous poem refers to the folk belief which persists in places to this day that the sun itself dances in the sky to celebrate the resurrection of the Christ:

> The Merry Sun on Easter Morn
>     Hoppeth and skippeth one two three
> For that Gods Son
> His Fair Foot putteth down
>     On greensward under Tree
>     Dancing right gladsomely
>     Out of Hell now to be
> And so be everyone. *Alleluia*.

In the dawn garden the Risen Christ encounters His love. There is a medieval Easter carol which begins:

> Tomorrow shall be my dancing day,
> I would my true love did so chance
> To see the measure of my play
> To call my true love to my dance.
> Sing O my love, O my love, my love, my love,
> This have I done for my true love.

'This' refers alike to His descent into the womb and into the tomb. His 'true love' is the human soul, represented in the gospel story by the Magdalen who comes to meet Him, searching for

## The Risen Body

Him as He has searched for her. She gropes blindly, not knowing Him, 'supposing Him to be the gardener'. He is indeed the 'gardener' of her soul. This scene is the most translucently beautiful image in the literature of the world of the metamorphosis of the soul in the moment of its abandonment to the Divine Love. Jesus speaks her Name:

'Mary.'

In all the traditions the name signifies the innermost being of the self. Here, the Christ Being utters the True Name of the Eternal Beloved. (At one time it was the custom for every Catholic, boy or girl, to be given the name 'Mary', as being the true Name of the human soul.) By that Name, with infinite tenderness and reassurance, God addresses Himself to the fallen soul whom He so loved that He entered the depths of the labyrinth and slew the Monster for her sake. Whereupon she *turns herself*.

'She turned herself and saith unto him, Rabboni, which is to say, Master.'

There is a world of meaning in this curious figure of speech. It is curious, because she had already spoken to Him and must have been facing Him when she did so. But still she *turns herself*. In fact the reference is to the ancient teaching that the process of passing into another dimension or another *time* is one of *turning* in a spiralling movement on the 'still point'. And now comes something stranger still. Mary would have sprung towards Him, impatient to kiss His hands and feet. But He motions her back.

*Noli me tangere*. ('Touch me not'.)

In explanation He adds: 'For I am not yet ascended to my Father.'

The Church has omitted to explain the explanation; although Christians, of course, have speculated endlessly on the subject. On the human level, the sexual overtones of the command are so obvious that no one can be unaware of them. But this is but the outer skin of the ineffable Mystery they suggest. The glorified Body of the Lord is a streaming flame of Fire. No one may touch It and live. This is not to say, however, that no one is to be permitted to touch the body of Jesus after its emergence from the tomb. Thomas is invited to do so, for instance. Jesus is capable, at any time, of withdrawing the glory into Himself. For Mary He will not do this; for Mary, since the Crucifixion, He is *mana* (untouchable in the sense of being sacrosanct on pain of death) until the Moment of their Reunion in Heaven at the End of Time. This untouchability of the Crucified Body in relation to Mary Magdalen has to do with her dual role as lover and as penitent. Her sins are forgiven, but they are not yet wiped out. She has yet to be purified in the Fire of His Love. (We have to remember, of course, that we are speaking of things which transcend the limitations of time: in reality there is no 'gap' between the successive 'episodes' of the Myth, but a single instantaneous Event.) In all the great religious traditions we come upon the idea that Absolute Holiness is not to be 'touched'. Only the totally pure can survive such a contact. Mary the Virgin can survive it; not Mary the Prostitute. For Thomas and the other disciples, the Lord is prepared to *withdraw*, so that what is presented for their handling is something far less than the Reality it represents. His encounter with Mary is *unveiled*, holding nothing back; and if we ask why, the answer can only be that Mary is His Heavenly Love. 'Before' the Crucifixion she could touch Him (we are told that she washed His feet and anointed them with precious ointments and wiped them with her flaming hair, symbol of her unlimited promiscuous sex). That is because the Lord's body is not *mana* until it has received the insignia of sin – the Five Wounds of the Passion which complete the manifestation of the Son of Man – and until it has been plunged in the Baptism of Fire at the heart of the earth, to emerge as the complete manifestation of Man, the Son of God. In relation to Mary He is, at each stage of the Myth, *all* that He is at that moment. From her He withholds nothing. But, between the Crucifixion and the Marriage in Heaven, Mary in her role as His Lover is not ready for His touch. The Assumption of the Virgin, when Christ, having 'ascended to the Father', draws Her bodily into Heaven to be crowned in the Mystery of the Trinity as the deified Church, is the reunification of the two Marys in the Heart of God. When this comes to pass (in the words of Meister Eckhart):

'At-oned with her creator the soul has lost her name for she herself does not exist: God has absorbed her into him just as the sunlight swallows up the dawn till it is gone.'

Redeemed humanity is *deified* in the two Marys. This redeemed and deified humanity is the Mystical Church, referred

## The Risen Body

to in the liturgy sometimes as the 'Bride', and sometimes as the 'Body' of the Christ. The two appellations appear to contradict one another, and are frequently taken to be little more than poetic fancies. But they have a very definite meaning. The Christ-body is essentially divine. It is that Body of Light which has Its Being eternally in God. At the same time It is human; and in that sense – although in that sense only – it is that part of the Divine-human Nature which is bestowed by Mary and represents Her Divinised Humanity or Man. Christ assumes Man's nature by assuming a human body in His Mother's womb. The early Fathers defined the two natures of the God-Man as being not *separate* but *distinct*. They exist, it is said, in a 'hypostatic union'; and it is this union of the two natures which is imaged for us first in the Moment of Conception in the Virgin's womb, finally in the Celestial Nuptials which *are* the assumption of our human nature into God. The *human* nature of Jesus is virtually identical with Mary, since He has no bodily father; His Father is pure Spirit ('I am the Child of Earth and Starry Heaven'): and Mary is the entirety of Creation gathered together in the Mystical Church.

These images and the meanings they represent are infinitely subtle but they are also and essentially *accurate*. To understand them we have to think ourselves into a state of mind in which it is possible to see that the Assumption of the Virgin into Heaven, the assumption of Mary's bodily nature by Jesus in the womb, and the Heavenly Nuptials in which Mary is at-oned with the Divine-Human, Spirit-Body of the Christ, are three modes of a single Event. Seeing this, we are able to look at this Event as it were from three points of view. Mary is the Mother and the Bride of God. And Mary is that human Body which God Himself puts on, in order that *we* may put it on a second time, renewed in Him. Again let us remind ourselves: *that Body is the Mystical Church*. Individually, we are Its members. But the members of Christ's Body are co-herent in One Will. They exist in a state of simplicity, carrying out their several functions in perfect co-ordination, in union with the Sacred Heart. In the Roman Catholic Church, the Sacred Heart of Jesus is presented, iconographically, as an object of worship. The Sacred Heart of Mary is invariably depicted as pierced by seven swords. These swords – paralleled in the 'seven devils' of the Magdalen –

represent Her sufferings upon earth, and Her joys in Heaven, where Her Heart is eternally pierced by the darts of the Love of God.

St Paul, speaking of our corporeal nature, wrote: 'It is sown a natural body; it is raised a spiritual body.' He meant that we undergo a metamorphosis in death. As the butterfly emerges from the chrysalis, so does the New Man in Christ arise out of the discarded garment of our mortal flesh. The bodies of Christ and of the Virgin are translated directly into Heaven (because they *are*, in Heaven); but we, having discarded our corrupted bodies and consigned them to the elements from which they came, will *put on* the Risen Body of the Lord. That is what is meant by 'the Resurrection of the body', in which Christians reaffirm their belief whenever they recite the Creed. Having died in Him, in Him we shall rise again. This is an *unimaginable state*. Most of us have to confess that Easter is the hardest for us to understand of all the great Festivals of the Church. It is the greatest of them all; and yet (unless we fall into the ever-present temptation of *sentimentalising* it to mean something which essentially it does not and cannot mean for us) we find ourselves more deeply moved on Christmas Day – and, indeed, on Good Friday, which is only too easily imagined and applied to ourselves. Easter represents our deification. This seems very far away and strange. It is not; but we have to become 'as little children' in order to see that it is not.

The Mystery of the Transfiguration has to do with the glorified Body, although it occurs in time 'before' the Crucifixion, and we are not told that Jesus permitted His Sacred Wounds to appear 'in anticipation' of the latter Event. The Lord, on the Mount of Transfiguration, reveals Himself to the three disciples who are closest to Him, more fully than on any other occasion recorded in the New Testament. He permits them, as it were, a foretaste of the Resurrection. In the Hindu scripture known as the *Bhagavad Gita*, the great Song of Praise to the Lord Krishna, the Son of God, Krishna, having previously concealed Himself under the appearance of a charioteer, appears suddenly 'in His glory' to His disciple Arjuna; and 'if the light of a thousand suns should suddenly burst forth it would be like unto the light of that exalted one'. Of Jesus we are told that 'his face did shine as the sun and his raiment was white . . . and behold there appeared unto them Moses and Elias talking with him'. Moses and Elias represent in this vision what Arjuna means when he declares: 'I see the gods in Thy body, O God, all of them.' The disciples 'fell on their faces and were sore afraid'. Arjuna, 'filled with amazement, his hair standing upright . . . bowed his head'. It is not often that one can make this kind of direct comparison between the scriptures of two widely differing traditions without risk of confusion; but here the similitude is apparent. Perhaps the most constant and unmistakable theme of all the great world religions is that of the Heavenly Beauty of the Representative of God (whether He be the Divine Son Himself, or the Enlightened One or the Messenger – or in whatever guise He appears in the Myth). He is more beautiful, they tell us, than the rising sun.

Beauty is the vesture of God. The Sufi mystic Ibn' Arabi declares that even love is not an end in itself – we love God for His Beauty. Christians would add that He bestows His Beauty upon us in the Risen Christ and loves us for That. Christ is the Perfect Rose. He is the Cosmic Flower unfolding from within, which expands to embrace all the worlds, and contracts again to withdraw them into Itself.

'I saw my Lord with the eye of my heart, and I said: Who art Thou? He said: Thou.' These words, taken from the writings of Al-Hallaj, another Sufi, reflect the dialogue between Jesus and Mary in the dawn garden. This dialogue represents the awakening of the soul. The garden is the heart of the lover of God.

Chapter Fourteen

# The Ascent of the Son and the Descent of the Spirit

As the Christ ascends into Heaven, the Spirit, passing through Him, descends upon the Church. Jesus said to His disciples: 'Unless I go the Comforter cannot come.' 'Comforter' here refers to the strengthening of their Communion with one another in Him. The Ascension is a two-way Movement passing eternally through Itself; so that by means of It the Seed of Christ is brought back into the world to fructify the Church and bring about its coinherence as the growing Body of the Lord (this operation being parallel to, and united with, that of the fructification of the Virgin's womb by the same Spirit).

That which ascends is the Risen Body of the Christ. It is His human body received from Mary. At the same time it is His Body of Light. These two ideas have to be very subtly and carefully distinguished. We have to be very sure that we are not slipping into the notion that *we* bestow upon God a substantiality which He would not otherwise possess. In the *Maitri Upanishad* it is written: 'Now that golden Person who is within the sun, who looks down upon this earth from His golden palace, is even He who dwells within the Lotus of the Heart and *eats food*.' When we read in the gospels that the Risen Lord *ate food*, we have a slight tendency to imagine that God as He is in Himself could not have done this! We assume, however unconsciously, that the substantiality of the Risen Body depended upon Its humanity, not realising that It was able to appear and disappear and to pass through doors and walls not because It was *less* substantial than those doors and walls but because they, in comparison with It, were insubstantial as a ghost. The last way in which to think of

## The Ascent of the Son and the Descent of the Spirit

Heaven is to visualise it as being an insubstantial state. The notion that Christ in His Divine-human Body forever dwells in some sort of ghostly 'spiritual' abode is an obvious nonsense; yet many Christians have, more or less unconsciously, entertained it. The Creed defines the Only Begotten Son as 'being of one *substance* with the Father'.

We live in a world which consists – *because it appears to us to consist* – of three dimensions continuously moving in time. The dimensions of Eternity are infinite, and time is one of them. Even we, however, if we put our minds to it, can see that a plane is more 'real' than a line, a cube than a plane, and (although this is a rather more difficult idea) a body extended in time than one which is continuously being 'lost' in an illusory 'present'. So the *more* dimensions we are capable of 'seeing', the more real and substantial is the world we experience. Meanwhile the dimensions we are unable to perceive *for us* are non-existent. To pass into another dimension is to *disappear*. The serial dimensions are the great impassibles of the universe: to realise this, we have only to imagine how a three-dimensional object passing at right angles through a two-dimensional surface, would, from the latter's point of view, undergo inexplicable changes and eventually *vanish*. In the Mystery of the Ascension the Lord *vanishes*. He lingers with His disciples forty days and then 'while they beheld He was taken up; and a cloud received him out of their sight'.

They no longer see Him; but they have His promise that He is with them still. The new manifestation of His Presence in the world is the Spirit Who descends from above, bearing with Him the New Seed, the Seed of the Church.

But *where*, they are asking, has He *gone*? He has not 'gone' anywhere, of course. But we, of necessity, ask this question; and the Christian tradition has answered it in the only way possible in terms of the dimensions we know. In those terms, we can only think of Heaven as being 'above' us. The idea of 'above' and 'below' as denoting the *distance* between our humanity and the Plenitude of God is so basic to our thinking that to rid ourselves of it is to rid ourselves of the knowledge that *there is such a distance*. And to be without this knowledge is to forget that we are no-thing before God. So we become deprived of the capacity for worship. We become deprived, before we know what is happening to us, even of the capacity to respect one another; since we can only do this by situating ourselves in a right relation to That which is above us all, the One from Whom alone we derive whatsoever there is in us which is worthy of respect. (And indeed we are the Sons of God, above all other creatures, for which cause the most seemingly outcast among us is in dignity as a king. For what, after all, is a king but a living symbol of the dignity of Everyman in Christ?) Of course there is here a blinding paradox. *There always is.* We shall not escape being caught upon paradox until we are free of the limitations imposed by our bondage to three-dimensionability and serial time – and the particular kind of logical thinking which those limitations necessitate.

To visualise Heaven as being 'up there' comes naturally to us, in any case, because it corresponds to the truth. Our physical universe is a *mode of perceiving* the universe of God. For Dante our earth was the 'mid-place' situated half way between Heaven and Hell, the former being represented by the firmament above our heads, the latter by the realms of impenetrable rock beneath our feet. This is not just a metaphor or 'symbol': it is actually the truth *as we perceive the truth*. The heavens above and the earth beneath are modes of our perceiving, and will remain so for as long as the limitations of that perceiving remain. Those limitations are the definition of our world. In Eternity all distance is abolished. Here, in this world, we have part in Eternity; and we know that God is closer to us than we are to ourselves: that knowledge is in itself Heaven; it is what the gentle Brother Lawrence described as 'the practice of the Presence of God'. But in so far as we continue to inhabit 'this world' we are subject to *distance*.

In medieval times, when the physical world was less sharply differentiated from the higher realities to which it corresponds, maps were drawn depicting the heavens as a series of concentric spheres, the idea being that the dwelling-place of the Most High was situated beyond those spheres; and meanwhile the spheres themselves were imagined as turning forever one upon the other with ecstatic sound. The spheres may be thought of as the serial dimensions, which can only open out before us as the process of our purification makes it possible for them to do so. We have already considered the association of *purity* with *passibility*. The

## The Ascent of the Son and the Descent of the Spirit

concentric spheres, or dimensions, are passible only to the pure in heart. Meanwhile it is the most natural – and, in the truest meaning of the word, *sensible* – thing in the world to associate the luminous serenity of the starry skies with the dwelling-place of God.

We began this meditation on the Ascension by defining It as being part of a two-way Movement. This idea may be further developed by means of the Blakean vision of a vortex rolling back. Blake describes an intimation of infinity which will help us to understand how the Coming of the Holy Spirit (or the coming-into-being of the Church) is *made way for* by the ascending passage of the Christ:

'The nature of infinity is this: that everything has its own vortex, and when once a traveller through Eternity has pass'd that vortex, he perceives it roll backward behind his path, into a globe itself unfolding like a sun.'

The Church is the Christ-Body of mankind. It comes into being as the rolling backward behind Him of His own passage through the multidimensional spirals of time and space. As it does so, it is *informed* by the Holy Spirit. The Spirit is that which implants the Seed of the new Christ-Body and enables it to grow. We have seen this in the Annunciation. Now we see it 'again'. Innumerable ritual objects and patterns, appearing in widely separated times and places, are totally incomprehensible until we understand them as representations of a vortex rolling back upon itself. The Tibetan dorje, shaped like an hour-glass or like a flower with alternate petals bent back upon the stem, is such an object. The Taj Mahal with its water-tank reflecting the image of perfect beauty upside down is another. St Peter, who was crucified upside down, represents the Church as the mirror image of the Christ. When the New Creation is complete it will be the perfect replica of the Old. In reality there is no distinction between the two.

A vortex has a spiralling movement. Blake's vortex is a whorl which becomes a globe. This idea of the spiralling vortex as being the nearest we can get to an accurate diagram of reality appears to be universal; it expresses itself in myth and symbol and visual work of art. Jack's beanstalk is a natural spiral; Jacob's ladder is a moving spiral staircase (with, be it noted, a *two-way* movement; angels are ascending and descending upon it). The

Magdalen *turns* towards Jesus. Alice, going through the looking-glass, *turns* into another dimension where everything is 'the other way round'. Christians are so used to repeating the words 'in Whom is no darkness neither shadow cast by turning' that they often fail to relate them either to the turning of our terrestrial globe towards and away from the sun, or to those more hidden and mysterious motions to which that turning corresponds. Tibetans ritually circumnambulate their holy places, as Muslims do the Ka'aba; and these circumnambulations are understood as being *spiral* movements because they occur *in time*. (Time moves in a direction imperceptible to us; and so with each turn of our circles we move on a spiralling path. Traditionally, the right-hand turn represents the *ascending*, the left the *descending* movement.) So we shall see things more truly if we visualise the Christ as ascending into Heaven along the axis of a whorl of Light. Only in Heaven itself does the 'whirling' cease, contained in the stillness of the Heart of God. 'In Whom is no darkness nor shadow cast by turning . . .'

The time which is traditionally believed to have elapsed between the Resurrection of the Lord and His Ascension is forty days, during which period it is supposed that He propounded to His disciples many of those secret teachings which were later incorporated in the Myth. Forty is a number esoterically associated with the 'life after death'. A few authoritative texts survive, originating in various parts of the world, relating in visionary language the experiences of the soul in this state. St Makary of Alexandria, writing in the third century, describes the wanderings of the soul for forty days between death and judgement. The Tibetan Book of the Dead speaks of this same length of time as passing between judgement and re-entry into the womb. There is here some meaning which eludes us. The most we can say is that clearly the period mentioned in the Gospels is strictly related to the mysteries of number and of time. It could not have been otherwise than forty days. When the time is accomplished Christ vanishes from the sight of His friends.

Ten days later, on the Jewish Feast of Weeks, 'they were all with one accord in one place. And suddenly there came a sound from heaven as of a rushing mighty wind and it filled all the house where they were sitting. And there appeared unto them cloven tongues as of fire and it sat upon each

## The Ascent of the Son and the Descent of the Spirit

one of them. And they were all filled with the Holy Ghost.'

Traditionally, although the Book of Acts does not say so, the 'one place' was the Upper Room of the Last Supper, another name for which is the Cenacle. Here there is a correspondence with the Virgin's womb, into which the Spirit descended in a previous cycle bearing the Seed of the Body of Christ. This time it is the Seed of the Church that He implants in the world. The sound of His Coming is that of the vortex created by the Ascent of the Lord. It swirls down from Heaven bearing the Seed which it gathered as It passed Him on the Way. Traditionally, Mary is seated in the centre of the room, encircled by the Twelve. 'Where the Holy Ghost Her Spouse has found Mary in a soul', wrote St Louis de Montfort, 'he flies there.' This is not a poetic fancy, but an accurate metaphysical statement. Mary is the magnet who attracts the Spirit. As Sophia, She performed this function at the Creation of the world. She performs it again in the initial moment of the Incarnation; and again at the founding of the Church. Blake has a passage in 'Jerusalem' which points to the connection between the Mystical Church and the Mother of God: 'There is a Void outside of Existence, which if entered into englobes itself and becomes a womb.' The womb of the Virgin is the Void which is penetrated by the Holy Spirit. Creation *ex nihilo* (out of nothing) is accomplished.

*Veni creator Spiritus* is the great Pentecostal cry of the Church. The Hymns to the Holy Spirit are all of them invocations, drawing Him down, imploring His rejuvenating grace. The sacraments are liturgical re-enactments of the two-way movement of ascent and descent. Christ is offered up; and the Spirit descends upon us in response. The reason for the stern prohibition against magical practices (even of an apparently 'harmless' or 'white' variety) within the Community of Christians is simply that magic is, by definition, the acquisition of power *without* the invocation of the Holy Spirit. (In fact, many so-called 'magical' practices *do* invoke the Spirit and *are* performed in the Name of Jesus Christ or in some other Name which refers to the Son of God; in such cases there is an organic connection with the regular sacraments of the Church, whether this is officially recognised or not. On the other hand, a great deal of the advanced technology of our own times is pure magic, and much of it 'black'.)

## The Christian Mystery

The disciples emerged from the Upper Room in a state of ecstasy; so that unsympathetic onlookers accused them of being drunk. This ecstasy took strange forms. We are told, for instance, that they 'spoke with tongues as the Spirit gave them utterance'.

Ecstasy, whether corporate or individual, has never been officially encouraged by the Church. In other, less rigidly institutionalised traditions it has been more openly and courageously admitted as a valid and even necessary part of the total religious experience at least for certain individuals and groups. Hysteria is another matter – this is a psychosomatic condition of passivity which can lead to diabolical possession in some cases. The Christian sacraments were originally instituted as appropriate channels for what are known as the charismatic Gifts. By means of the sacraments, when these are being properly used, the higher realities to which they correspond are enabled to flow downwards, transforming everything in their path. In the course of this operation all kinds of experiences may take place. The law of correspondence ensures that higher level states are being constantly reflected *lower down* in the scale of existence. What has to be realised is that the lower levels can *resemble* the higher without there being, of necessity, any thread of communication remaining between the two, so that what appear on the surface to be similar phenomena may in fact be entirely different. The higher contains the lower; but the lower does not automatically lead to the higher; and nothing can be more dangerous than the attribution of spiritual validity to low-level experiences of a purely psychosomatic nature, on account of a superficial resemblance. St Teresa of Avila was so conscious of this danger in her own case (and was so severely treated by her confessor, who represented the official attitude of the Church) that she suffered unnecessary anguish for years, continually probing her conscience for fear lest her genuine experiences should prove to be false.

The spiritual friend of St Teresa was St John of the Cross. ('Spiritual friendship' is a term denoting one of the most beautiful relationships in the world, that between a man and a woman who would normally have been lovers, but whose sexuality has been fulfilled in the Love of God.) He seems to have been less troubled by scrupulosity. In poem after poem he

*The Ascent of the Son and the Descent of the Spirit*
testifies to the ineffable sweetness and ecstasy of the mystical experience:

> I entered in, I know not where,
> And I remained, though knowing naught,
> Transcending knowledge with my thought.
>
> So borne aloft, so drunken-reeling,
> So rapt was I, so swept away,
> Within the scope of sense and feeling
> My sense or feeling could not stay.
> And in my soul I felt, revealing,
> A sense that, though its sense was naught,
> Transcended knowledge with my thought . . .
>
> If you would ask, what is its essence –
> This summit of all sense and knowing:
> It comes from the Divinest Presence –
> The sudden sense of Him outflowing,
> In His great clemency bestowing
> The gift that leaves men knowing naught,
> Yet passing knowledge with their thought . . .

In our own day, the Hindu Swami Ramdas has summed up the effects of being (as Christians would say) filled with the Holy Spirit:

'When the source of immortal joy is opened within us, it flows and saturates every fibre of our being, internal and external, and makes our life at once a waveless peace and a ceaseless thrill of ecstasy. Death, fear and grief have then no significance for us.'

One could continue indefinitely with similar quotations describing the raptures of the saints. Yet there have been many who, like Therese of Lisieux, attained to an extraordinary degree of communion with God without any sensible or emotional experiences at all. This fact is consistent with the teaching (fully recognised by all the great mystics, and exquisitely analysed by St John of the Cross) that God must ultimately be known to us in Darkness because we could not endure the blinding radiance of His Light.

## Chapter Fifteen

# *Our Lady in Heaven*

The Holy Virgin does not die but *falls asleep*. And once again the Event takes place in the Upper Room. The Twelve Apostles are present. It is said that they carried Her sleeping body to the summit of a hill, from which it was assumed into Heaven. In many paintings of the Dormition, Christ is represented as descending along a shaft of Light to carry away His Mother in His arms. This must be seen as the 'repetition' of His descent into Her womb. As always it is, in a sense, the same Event. The Holy Spirit descends upon Mary bearing with Him the Christ. The fulfilling of Mary with the Love of God is both Her Impregnation and Her Assumption into the Presence of that Love. The scene may be the Cenacle or the summit of a hill – or the 'garden enclosed' of the Annunciation and the Song of Songs, or the tiny room opening out of that garden, beloved of the Italian Renaissance. All of these backgrounds are but images of the human soul in the moment of its visitation by the Spirit: the Cenacle is the enclosing principle of material form pierced by the Divine Shaft; the enclosed garden is the purified heart of the saint; the summit of the hill is the apex into which all the lower levels of being are caught up in the moment of metamorphosis into Everlasting Life.

The Virgin is caught up into Heaven in order to be crowned as its Queen by virtue of Her Nuptials with the Son. In a number of paintings of the Assumption – for instance, the famous one by Matteo Giovanni in the National Gallery, London – Her girdle is depicted as falling from Her waist (to be caught by one of the disciples, who represent the Church-in-time, awaiting the consummation at the Last Day). This obvious piece of symbolism is one of the many oblique references to the Divine Nuptials

## Our Lady in Heaven

which occur in traditional art. Another is the ubiquitous representation of the Infant Jesus placing a ring on the finger of St Catherine, who (in identification with this Mystery) dreamed of her Betrothal to the Christ. (She was not alone in being granted the privilege of this dream: like the stigmata of St Francis, it is an example of what has already been referred to as 'role-playing' on the part of the saints.)

The Shaikh Al-Arabi Ad-Darquawi wrote:

'Now if God wishes to sanctify one of His servants, He marries Spirit and soul within him.'

This Sufic saying has a bearing upon the Mystery of the Holy Virgin in Her Nuptials with God. As God is to man, Spirit is to soul, man is to woman: this pattern of symbolism is basic to the Christian tradition, and is by no means peculiar to that tradition. So Mary is the soul of Man or (since the whole of creation is held to be contained within Man) the soul of the World; and the Spirit of God is Her Divine Spouse. Yet Mary is the Church; and the Church is the Bride of Christ. Dante apostrophises the Queen of Heaven as 'Virginal Mother, Daughter of thy Son'. So the point of view constantly changes; but there is no inconsistency in these changing aspects of the Marian role. The Holy Spirit is Her Spouse in the sense that He impregnates Her womb with the Seed which is the Christ. Strictly speaking, He is the Spouse of the earth-dwelling Virgin; while Her Nuptials in Heaven with the Divine Son represent Her Apotheosis as the Eternal Woman, 'Our Lady' as the Church calls Her, the Principle of Femininity in the Godhead, Who is only not-God because She has been *deified by* Him, being no-thing in Herself. As Sophia She arose from the Void in response to the Word (it is in this sense that She is 'Daughter of thy Son'). This represents the Beginning of a Great Cycle. Her Nuptials represent the End. But there is, in reality, no 'beginning' and no 'end'; for it is from those Nuptials at the consummation of a 'time' that a New Time is born; and so in Eternity there is forever a coming-to-be and a death and a coming-together in Love. The destiny of each individual soul and the destiny of the whole created world are contained within this Movement whereby Love forever re-creates Itself.

The Book of the Revelation of St John, which contains, under some of the strangest and most esoteric imagery to be found in the Bible, a description of the rolling up of time at the Last Day,

## The Christian Mystery

is a terrifying document; and yet it contains whole chapters so moving and beautiful that no sensitive person can read them and not weep. It describes the New Heaven and the New Earth presided over by the Spirit and the Bride:

'And I saw a new heaven and a new earth: for the first heaven and the first earth were passed away; and there was no more sea. And I John saw the holy city, new Jerusalem, coming down from God out of heaven saying, Behold the tabernacle of God is with men . . . and there shall be no more death, neither sorrow nor crying, neither shall there be any more pain: for the former things are passed away . . . Behold I make all things new . . .'

There is a suggestion here of the Ultimate Mystery: that beyond the cycles of time in which life and death continuously move in and out of one another, and Creation arises in the Void and is sustained by the Cross – beyond these things is the moveless Blessedness of God which will 'never again' become involved in sin and in suffering and in death. This is the final, although to us incomprehensible, truth. And meanwhile Mary, the Bride, is 'the perfect mediator between heaven and earth'. This phrase describing Her is taken from the Jewish scripture known as the Zohar, a post-Christian document which emerged in thirteenth-century Spain as a kind of compendium of Jewish esotericism heavily impregnated with Christian and Sufic elements. It relates to *Shekinah*, not specifically to Mary; but the two Names are interchangeable for anyone who understands the inner meaning of the two intertwined traditions to which they respectively belong. The whole passage reads as follows:

'Above all the angels is placed the Matrona or Shekinah, who looks after the palace of the Supreme King . . . Know that the road that leads to the Tree of Life is the Matrona. All the messages that the Supreme King sends below must pass through her hands first. And all the messages from this world to the Supreme King come to her and she transmits them. She is the perfect mediator between heaven and earth.'

Pope Pius XII, at the time of his death, was preparing to respond to a popular demand, consistently encouraged throughout his pontificate, virtually to affirm the deification of the Virgin by formally declaring Her to be 'Mediatrix of all graces' and 'Co-Redemptress' with Her Son. Since then a reaction has set in. But, had these pronouncements been made, they would

## Our Lady in Heaven

have represented nothing more than the logical conclusion of the doctrine of the Blessed Virgin Mary and Her role. (This conclusion had, of course, been accepted from the beginning and consistently taught: it was simply a question of formalising it as *de fide*: of the Faith.) If She be not in Heaven, the soul of Everyman is lost. For She *is* the soul of Everyman in Heaven. And here in 'our world' the soul can aspire to be only that which essentially it is.

A positive mountain of confusion would be avoided if only we could realise what is meant, esoterically, by the identification of Our Lady in Heaven with the Mystical Church. The most awe-inspiring – and, in its abuse, appalling – doctrine of the Church of Rome (now inevitably discarded at the cost of losing the entirety of the meaning it represents) is contained in the words *Extra Ecclesiam nulla salus*: 'Outside the Church is no salvation'. This is not only true: it is an essential component of the Myth. But only, of course, when one understands the meaning of Our Lady and the meaning of the Church. One can but repeat it again, and yet again: the Church in Eternity is Everyman in Christ. In what sense the historic institution, broken and divided as it is and representing in any case only a fraction of mankind, has the right to claim identity with the Mystical Body, is so subtle and paradoxical that Christians can hardly be blamed for having misinterpreted it. Understanding can only come slowly, as we learn to free our minds from the categories of either or which tend to dominate our thoughts. There is an ancient saying, the origin of which is not known: 'This also is Thou; neither is this Thou.' The Christ Mystery rests upon this conundrum. The whole world rests upon it. It is the riddle of how that which is not can *be*, and that which *is* can be that which is not. The answer to it is that out of no-thing the Lord creates the heavens and the earth. And if this seems a far flight from the question of the status of the Church-in-time, it can only be said that until we can begin to see the answer to the riddle, the question of the Church-in-time can only be answered, on one side or the other, in a way that is disastrously false.

We are shown in the Christ-Mystery that the metaphysical centre is at-oned with every point on the circumference. So every possible kind of human society, provided only that it is oriented towards God and derives its co-herence from Him

## The Christian Mystery

(and if it does not, it will be found to be lacking in the very principle of co-herence) is at-oned with Christ. The Church is a society of this sort; more, it is, even in its earthly manifestation, for its members the archetype of them all. There may be – indeed there must be – in the Christian society many 'churches', so to speak, within the Church. (The family unit is one of them; the kingdom is another; the parish is a third – one could go on indefinitely listing the units or types which derive both their justification and their pattern from the Whole.) The Spirit descends upon the Centre, which is, mysteriously, the centre of *each one*: for this is a multidimensional figure that we are trying to understand, a figure in which the Centre of the World is the centre of the heart and of every coherent unit within the church. These things are not 'images' merely; they are true. But here it is necessary to pause; since human society is not unified in the way we are seeing it in the Myth. There is one Truth, but there are many and even apparently diverse ways of expressing that Truth. There are, bewilderingly, *many myths*. There are many and widely differing societies which claim to be what Christians mean when they speak of 'the Church'; and they make this claim in terms, and using patterns of imagery, which are often very far removed from the Christian mythology, and cannot easily be brought into a meaningful relationship with it.

This situation is an aspect of our total situation in a fallen world. It is so hard to understand that, at this point, we shall leave it; for a moment comes when the stringing of words upon words is no longer any use. A moment comes when we can *only* understand by retreating into that place where all things become simple in the Presence of God.

## Chapter Sixteen

# *The Last Things*

'The Four Last Things', in traditional Catholic terminology, are Death, Judgement, Hell and Heaven. Purgatory, which is held to be by far the most common state to be entered immediately after death, is not included as a fifth. *Purgatory is a process in time*. The Four Last Things are Events occurring in a 'split second' at the End of Time. Whatever is 'beyond' them is beyond time itself.

It is on account of the prominence given to this aspect of its tradition, that the Church has been accused of being almost exclusively interested in 'the life after death'. This is not the case. The Myth of the life after death, while purporting to be valid as such, is applicable to every moment of life *because our world is the intersection in time of all the levels and all the states*. Death, Judgement, Hell and Heaven are here and now. They cut through the lines of our times, those lines which have been designated 'purgatory' in the Myth. (Purgatory or time is the state in which man cannot *choose*, but can only suffer the results of the choices he has made and by which he is being judged.) The relationship between eternity and time, although we experience it in our lives, is virtually impossible to grasp with our minds except in these mythical terms: so in the Four Last Things we are shown both the 'life after death' and the life we are living in this world, in such a way that no absolute division can be made between the two.

Every great world religion puts forward a 'scheme' of the soul's journeyings in the realms 'beyond death'. The Christian account is briefer than many of the others and, on the face of it, very different. It tells us nothing of those 'worlds' called by Tibetans the *Bardo*, in which the soul wanders amid illusions, passing from one stage to another and returning finally to 'this world', unless it has been strong enough to abjure the attraction which calls it back. Christianity speaks to us neither of 'reincarnation' nor of that stranger and more secret teaching of Eternal Recurrence, which suggests that a single life must be thoroughly 'worked out' before we pass on to the next stage of our existence. This does not, as is commonly supposed, imply that such teachings are *denied* by the Church. (As a matter of history, they have been, of course: but this need not necessarily have been so; as usual, such angry denials resulted from an undue exteriorisation of the Myth.) The Christian tradition *disregards* the 'adventures' (so to call them) of the discarnate – or for that matter, reincarnated – soul in the interval between death and judgement. It is interested solely in the End. It asks simply whether or not that soul is to be 'saved'. Therefore it is concerned exclusively with *final states*.

The soul passes into Eternity in the moment of death. At this point it is instructive to compare the Christian tradition in some detail with that of the *Bardo*, in order to see how the difference between the two is in the area of their primary concern, not in any point of 'belief'. Both traditions affirm that the soul, in this encounter with eternity, is momentarily blinded by the purity and radiance of the One Undivided and Absolute Truth. The *Bardo* calls this the experience of the 'white light'. Both traditions affirm that the vast majority of souls, unable to endure this encounter, pass on. The *Bardo*, written in the form of an instruction to be read aloud to the dying person, exhorts him *not* to do so; but then, assuming him to be unable to pay heed to this advice, it proceeds to describe in great detail the experiences he must now expect. These experiences are exceedingly complicated, painful and prolonged. They lead up to a reincarnation, which will in its turn lead on to a further cycle of wanderings in the *Bardo* realm; and so the cycles will continue until, after aeons of time, the purified soul is prepared to enter Heaven (or Nirvana) of its own choice. It is these experiences, including the successive 'reincarnations', which are simply telescoped as 'Purgatory' and left undescribed by the Church.

According to the Christian tradition, the saint is, by definition, the one who is sufficiently purified and humble to endure the Pure Light and pass instantaneously into the Presence of God. In this 'moment of eternity', which is not in fact subsequent to death but *is* death itself, the soul passes judgement on itself. It *chooses* its own place. So death, choice, judgement, Hell and Heaven, coinhere in one moment. This moment is (once more) the 'intersection of the timeless with time': it cuts through our world and our individual lives at every point in our passage through time, and supremely in the moment of death, which is the passage *out* of time, after which (for all but the saints) time turns round in a circle and recurs – in 'Purgatory', in the *Bardo*, we may call it what we will. But the Christian tradition is less concerned with the soul's adventures in time than with how it may extricate itself from them. So the Church prescribes exercises and prayers whereby Christians may assist one another to pass through the state of being *subject to time*.

Here then is the explanation of those odd-seeming little notices which used to be found on the prayer-desks of Catholic churches all over the world. Beneath a printed prayer would be written '100 days' or '30 days' or whatever, as the case might be. Every instructed Catholic understood what this meant. The Church, by virtue of its divinely bestowed authority, guaranteed that this number of 'days' would be subtracted from the purgatorial 'time' of whoever repeated the prayer in humility, penitence and faith. These arrangements, after centuries of misuse, had turned into a sort of inter-level banking system with 'merits' as the coin of exchange. The 'merits' (convertible into 'days') could be prayed for and applied to oneself or one's friends. One's own 'merits' (if one had any) could likewise be given away if one chose to be so charitable – or improvident. Beneath it all was the infinitely beautiful and glorious truth of the coinherence of all men in Christ. Sadly, this tended to become obscured. The system of 'indulgences', as it was called, reaching its logical conclusion in the actual buying and selling of 'merits', which was a world-wide trading enterprise in the heyday of the medieval Church, had eventually to go. The tragedy is that the truth which lay behind it is in danger of being lost as a result. This is what happens when the esotericism is forgotten and the exotericism runs riot.

A problem arises – again as a result of the esotericism being forgotten – when we come to the distinction normally made by Catholics between the Final and the 'particular' judgement. The

Final Judgement is the rolling up of time at the end of the Great Cycle on the Last Day. It is then that Christ Himself will re-turn in the Event known as the Second Coming of the Lord. Purgatory and this earth will fade away; and all the souls belonging to the completed cycle of time will be allotted their final places in Heaven or in Hell. The 'particular' judgement is the verdict passed upon each soul (or the *choice* made by each soul – there is in reality no difference between the two) in the moment of its passage through death: thus, after the 'particular' judgement, a soul which does not pass directly into Heaven or Hell will enter the state of Purgatory, where it will remain until the Last Day. And this too is confusing, exoterically, in view of the teaching that souls can shorten their 'time' in Purgatory by means of prayer and good works in this life. So, we may be tempted to ask, how is it then that we are all of us in Purgatory until 'the end of time', no matter how many good works we perform and pious prayers we recite? And of course all such questions are absurd. The final and the 'particular' Judgement are two *aspects* of One Moment.

The Church has never hesitated to emphasise the terrors of the Day of Judgement. In all the religious traditions, the preliminaries to the ultimate cataclysm of the rolling up of time are depicted as unrelievedly horrific. Time, it is implied, goes into spasms as it dies. Jesus spoke of 'signs in the sun and the moon and in the stars, and upon the earth distress of nations, the sea and the waves roaring, men's hearts failing them for fear and for looking after those things which are coming on the earth'. It is totally unrealistic to imagine that *any* religious tradition, least of all Christianity, which is centred upon the Mystery of Crucifixion, will relieve us of the element of horror as one aspect of our human existence. The horror will be metamorphosed into joy. But we have to encounter it first, as Jesus encountered it on the Cross.

This is perhaps more true, or at least more universally and communally true, at the present time than it has ever been before in the recorded history of mankind; since all the traditions are agreed that we are living in what the Hindus call the *Kali Yuga* (called by Christians 'the last days') when materialism, atheism and violence become predominant, a delicate balance is destroyed, and time seems to race forwards and downwards in a vertiginous plunge. Jesus said: 'When ye see these things come to pass know ye that the Kingdom of God is at hand.' There is no question here of 'evolution', no gradual or sudden 'improvement', but the expectation of a cataclysmic *change*. Disaster, tribulation, the apparent triumph of evil over good; and then, instantaneously, the total disappearance of our 'time' and the Second Advent of the Christ. (This does not mean that the concept of evolution is intrinsically false. The point is that we live in a 'falling' time. Evolution takes place, and is continuously distorted in the process. A simple illustration is the invention of the flying machine and our forays to the moon. These developments are a distortion of the levitational and astral 'skills' which could and would have accompanied that advanced stage of spiritual development which our present age was 'intended' to represent.)

The Coming of the Kingdom is anticipated in the Sabbath Day. The reason why it is natural for men to have a rest day, which is also a holy-day set aside for worship, is that this interval or day-out-of-time corresponds to the Day of Eternity which intervenes between the End of one Cycle and the Beginning of the next. Time and creation bring sorrow. Blake saw a vision of this when he painted the Elohim creating the Adam, the Winged Father hovering above the tortured form of the First Man, who lies outstretched upon a barren rock, his arms splayed out, blood spurting from the palms of his hands. In this painting Adam himself is identified with the crucified Christ.

As for death itself, its meaning is summed up in the words of the *Gita*, spoken by the Lord Krishna to His disciple:

'Whoso departeth thinking only of Me, without doubt goeth unto Me.'

Christianity, in common with the other great world religions, attaches primary importance to the state of the soul in the 'split second' of its departure from this world. This 'split second' is equivalent to the entirety of the life that has gone before. It is the soul's choice. The 'Pure Land' School of Buddhism teaches that 'all sentient beings' who call upon the sacred Name of Amida in that moment will be born into His Pure Land, no matter what may have been their sins. 'Today', said the Crucified Lord to the good-for-nothing criminal who turned to Him in faith, 'thou shalt be with me in Paradise' (and St Dismas, as he has since been

## The Christian Mystery

called, is therefore numbered with the saints and his festival observed throughout the Church). All Catholics are familiar with the phrase 'between the saddle and the ground'. It is used to express the idea that even the most hardened sinner, by an act of pure contrition uttered on his last breath (the image of a rider falling fatally from his runaway horse is intentionally appropriate) will be instantly translated into the Presence of God, without any need for Purgatory or punishment. An 'act of pure contrition' implies a degree of simplicity, humility and trust which most of us lack – but that is 'all' that it implies: moral 'worthiness' is beside the point.

The Church does not celebrate death. It expects that the mourners should wear black. Rejoicing is reserved for the anniversaries of the deaths of the saints. Up till very recent times (for now of course, temporarily at least, a great many traditional practices based upon an esotericism no longer understood, have been abolished) the Latin hymn known as the *Dies Irae* was said or sung at every Requiem Mass. The sonorous and terrifying syllables beat their way into the listeners' hearts:

> Dies irae dies illa
> Solvet saeculum in favilla
> Teste David cum Sibylla . . .

Paradoxically, it is true to say that one understands it better in Latin, whether one is acquainted with that language or not, than when it has been translated into English. In a hymn of this order the actual sound of the words and music is inseparable from the sense. In English it sounds merely gruesome and melodramatic:

> Day of wrath and terror looming,
> Heaven and earth to ash consuming –
> Seers and Psalmists true foredooming . . .

There are eighteen verses of it, without a light breaking through until the end, a cry torn from the heart of the dying in their consciousness of having so often turned from God. The end is hope; but hope in the infinite tenderness of Christ towards the sinner whose only merit is repentance:

> Pie Jesu Domine,
> Dona eis requiem. Amen.

## The Last Things

The old Anglican Burial service is equally awesome – and even more beautiful perhaps. As the coffin is about to be lowered into the grave, the priest says these words:

'Man that is born of a woman hath but a short time to live and is full of misery. He cometh up, and is cut down like a flower; he fleeth as it were a shadow, and never continueth in one stay. In the midst of life we are in death. Of whom may we seek for succour, but of thee O Lord, who for our sins art justly displeased? Yet O God most holy, O Lord most mighty, O holy and merciful Saviour, thou most worthy Judge eternal, suffer us not at our last hour for any pains of death to fall from thee.'

When the coffin is lowered earth is cast upon it. The priest says: 'Forasmuch as it hath pleased Almighty God of his great mercy to take unto Himself the soul of our dear brother (sister) here departed, we therefore commit his (her) body to the ground, earth to earth, ashes to ashes, dust to dust, in sure and certain hope of the Resurrection to eternal life through our Lord Jesus Christ; who shall change our vile body, that it may be like unto his glorious body, according to the mighty working whereby he is able to subdue all things to himself.'

Finally there is said or sung:

'I heard a voice from heaven saying unto me: Write, from henceforth blessed are the dead which die in the Lord; even so, saith the Spirit, for they rest from their labours.'

In our hearts we are not really consoled by anything less than the truth about our 'this worldly' state. We understand about death, even when the Prayer Book is altered and the parson tries to cheer us up. How could we not understand? The ancient scriptures of the Zoroastrians find an echo in our hearts: 'For three days and nights the soul sits beside the pillow of the body. And on the fourth day at dawn the soul will reach the lofty and awful Cinvat Bridge to which every man must come.' As the old carol for All Hallows E'en expresses it: 'To Brig o' Dread thou com'st at last, and Christe receive thy saule.' The 'Brig' comes first; and we must pass over it. In a Mystery it too is Christ; but that Mystery is not easily understood.

The Church has never actually said that we do not 'come back'. The myth (or 'doctrine' if the expression is preferred) of Purgatory covers an infinity of 'reincarnations' if we choose to believe in reincarnation; however, the truth is that to mix up our

## The Christian Mystery

own Myth with others does not get us very far in terms of advancement in the spiritual life, which demands an ever-increasing simplicity of heart, rather than brain-twisting efforts to live by a multiplicity of 'systems' all at once. It is true that on the esoteric level a total reconciliation is possible; but the intellectual exercise of finding it could take up all our lives: and there is no need; it is enough to know that such a possibility exists. Oriental teachings about reincarnation do not 'fit' at all easily into the Christian Myth, on the exoteric level at least. On that level they would, if introduced, deflect attention from what, in the Christian tradition, is (quite literally) the point.

On the other hand, it is difficult to leave the subject of what is so often and so misleadingly described as the 'after life', without mentioning (if only in passing) a teaching which lies behind the traditions of East and West alike. This teaching is one of the most ancient in the world. Its character is wholly esoteric, with the result that it is scarcely ever mentioned, even in the most profound texts, except in an oblique manner, in tantalising hints. In our own times it has been taught in the Gurdjieff-Ouspensky Schools as the 'theory of Eternal Recurrence'. Briefly, it is the theory that, since the moment of conception and the moment of death are eternal and one and the same, the soul *re-enters* the same life again and again until, after ages of ages, it has worked out the purpose of that life, perfected it and re-turned it to God. Exoterically understood, this teaching is too frightening to contemplate. Its suggestion of 'again and again' is rejected with disgust. (This is particularly so, of course, if the life in question has been more than usually unhappy or deprived.) Esoterically understood, its meaning is revealed as being totally unexpected and unlike its superficial appearance. There is really no question of 'again and again', but of *one life* which *changes*; and so, from a terrifying prospect, the teaching opens out into vistas of hope. It is a Myth: of course. But of all the myths of the soul's journey it is perhaps the nearest to a pure metaphysical statement. For those Christians who need it, it is Christian. By those who do not need it, it is unlikely to be even remotely understood.

## Chapter Seventeen

# *The World as Sacrament*

The Christian Mystery is the Mystery of the World as Sacrament.

To understand what this means we have to find a way of looking at 'this world' which sees it as the *meeting-place* between God and man – and between the two Eternal Movements of Love within the Godhead Itself. Man is created and sustained by those Movements. They may be called the Descending Word and the Ascending Sophia (or Spirit of the World); equally they may be called the Descending Spirit and the Ascending Christ. At the point of their Meeting Man *is*.

Man is being *drawn up* from the Abyss. He hangs between Being and Non-being, splayed out upon the Cross which can only be held together by the Love of God. No-thing presses upon him on all sides. At the same time the Love of God englobes him. No-thing is overcome; and man soars upwards with the Ascending Christ. He soars through many levels or 'worlds', all of which are contained within himself. It will help us to understand this if we make a distinction between three of these 'worlds' and see how they interpenetrate one another, and how all of them are present in 'this world' in a pattern of shifting relationships. Our three 'worlds', then, are the realm of Heavenly Light, the realm of Man, and the realm of Nature, which last may be subdivided, of course, in innumerable ways. Man is the connecting link between the highest and the lowest of the three. The realm of Nature, every subdivision of which is contained within man, is raised up by him into God. This *raising up* of creation from the Void is the priestly vocation of the Son of Man. He performs it in union with the Son of God. But still, as he does so, he is ceaselessly in danger of *falling back* into the Abyss. The Christ-Myth presents us with the idea that he 'did' originally fall back; so that now, as he is in the time-process of being 'rescued' by the Divine Son, his falling and his rising *coexist*. This is a difficult thought for us to hold in the mind; but it has to be grasped. The whole of Creation is at the same time rising and falling in a double movement.

In the track of Man's fall, the lower levels are dragged down. That is why, when we are angry, it comes naturally to our lips to insult one another with such epithets as 'You cat!' or 'You pig!' or simply 'You beast!' We talk about 'bestial' behaviour, knowing that the beasts themselves are not guilty of what we mean by this. George Macdonald, in his wise and beautiful novel *The Princess and Curdie*, describes the magical transformation of a group of human beings into bestial shapes, presenting these 'animals' as disgusting creatures, each one the embodiment of the predominant vice of the individual it represents. All this is confusing, until we understand that nothing in Nature is, or could possibly be, in any way unpleasant until it has been *dragged down* in the Fall of Man, so that every level is forced to identify itself with the one beneath. Man is not permitted to *identify* himself with his animal nature. In doing so, he degrades that nature. When a man is degraded to the level of a pig, he is gluttonous, dirty, cruel and sly. An actual pig is not like this. Essentially a peaceful, dignified, humourous creature, he looks upwards, in his own way, in the direction of man, as flowers look towards the sun. Man, by treating him with respect, draws out of him those aspects of human nature in which he naturally participates and which, in the animal realm, he is destined to represent. On the other hand, by mistreating him, man degrades him to the level of those vices which are the reverse aspect of the virtues he would normally possess. Meanwhile he himself remains *innocent*. Everything in Nature that is imperfect, including the very laws of its existence whereby it preys upon itself, has been made so by the choice of man. It is made so, out of time, in the Luciferian and Adamic Fall. In Lucifer it is the intellectual apex of man's nature that initiates the Fall. That is why his lower nature, that nature which now englobes him (as he was intended to englobe it) and appears as his environment, remains beautiful and innocent, held in a trembling balance between the opposites, in harmony – albeit a fearful harmony, ravaged by pain – with itself and with God.

## The World as Sacrament

So we return to the idea of the world as sacrament. Meister Eckhart declares: 'Every single creature has, in human nature, a stake in the Eternal.' In this passage he is referring not only to living creatures such as animals and plants. Rumi states the matter still more clearly in the beautiful words: 'When the seas of Mercy begin to surge, even the stones drink the Water of Life.' In the Eucharist, the Sacrament of the bread and the wine, the corn and the grapes, the whole of Nature is being carried up to God; for the earth is in the corn and the stones are in the earth. This all-embracing Sacrament, in which the lesser sacraments are all contained, is based upon the law of correspondence, whereby every level or realm of creation corresponds to the one above it by reflecting, in its own modes, the higher operations and forms – which are thereby mirrored in an infinite number of ways wherever one looks. 'As above so below' is a saying so ancient that we do not know its original source. In the *Vedas* we read: 'Yonder world is in the likeness of this world; and this world is in the likeness of that.' And the *Zohar* tells us: 'God made this terrestrial world in the image of the world above.' Hermes Trismegistus challenges us in these words: 'Do you say that God is invisible? Speak not so. Who is more manifest than God?' So, in more far-seeing times, scientists were members of an Order of Initiates who studied the physical world with the object of penetrating the Divine Mysteries, and finding therein the secret of man's origin and end. And meanwhile, embodied in a proliferating variety of religious rites, the cycle of the harvest, beginning with the ploughing of the earth and ending with the transmutation of the eaten fruit, was celebrated as the mirror image of the metaphysical fact of man's relationship with God. Physics itself is a myth of metaphysical truth. So is astronomy; and so now astrophysics. So is every aspect of our human experience. At the same time we dare not forget that, as has already been pointed out, every aspect of that experience has a *double face*.

There is a traditional Jewish prayer for recitation on the Sabbath Day: 'Blessed art thou, O Lord, who hast made a distinction between the Sacred and the Profane'. A distinction is not a separation; it is not a difference. What is meant here is that we need to clear a space at the centre of our lives, into which we bring *only that which has been dedicated to God*. This is done not with the purpose of desacralising the rest of the world, but with that of establishing a focal point from which holiness may spread out into the world. In a sense the operation is 'merely' formal and symbolic. But the fact, which it is utter folly to deny (and no one until recent times has seriously attempted to do so) is that our world, as we know it, is essentially ambivalent. Chaos and non-being have been permitted to enter our world. They will run amok if we do not hold them back. We do this *from the metaphysical centre*, the place of the heart. This is symbolised for us by the altar in the midst of the sanctuary, the Holy Table in the Holy Place. To this altar we *formally* bring back God's world and re-turn it to Him.

In the words of Black Elk, Chief and Wise Man of the Ogala Sioux:

'In setting up the sun dance lodge we are really making the universe in a likeness; for, you see, each of the posts around the lodge represents some particular object of creation, so that the whole circle is the entire creation, and the one tree at the center, upon which the twenty-eight poles rest, is *Waken Tanka*, who is the center of everything. Everything comes from him, and everything returns to him sooner or later . . . These are the things that are good for men to know and to remember.'

The Catholic Church has instituted seven sacraments. These are: Baptism, Confirmation, Order, Matrimony, Penance, Extreme Unction – and, central to them all, the Holy Eucharist, the solemn re-member-ance of the Body of Christ. The Anglican Prayer Book defines a sacrament as 'the outward and visible sign of an inward and spiritual grace'. The 'little red catechism' of Rome says substantially the same, adding in its oddly legalistic phraseology that 'the sacraments have the power of giving grace from the merits of Christ's Precious Blood which they apply to our souls'. The point being made is that the sacraments are *means* whereby the Power of the Holy Spirit is received and appropriated by men. There is no suggestion that they 'work' in a mechanistic fashion regardless of the state of mind of the recipient. They are formally recognised and accepted *meeting-points*.

In a valid sacrament three factors must be present. These are matter, action and intention. There has to be, in each case, *material* for the sacrament. This is chosen on the basis of the law

## The World as Sacrament

of correspondence. It is *acted upon* and it *acts upon* the participants, in whom there must be an *intention* to carry out the *intention* of the Church. This word 'intention', in traditional Catholic terminology, signifies the desire of the heart. It is used a great deal, and is enormously important. Where these three factors are present, the sacrament is completed by an Act of God. The Spirit descends upon matter, drawing it heavenwards in man. It descends upon man, drawing matter heavenwards in him. Every level of creation is involved. In a series of concentric circles the power flows outwards and is re-turned. In a sense there is only one Sacrament: the bread and the wine; the Body and the Blood. There is no need for anything else. The other sacraments were instituted as a more or less arbitrary breaking up into 'aspects' of the One.

The Holy Eucharist is the Sacrament of our Fellowship in Christ. As the life is drawn upwards from the stones, worked upon in co-operation by men, eaten in fellowship – and before being eaten offered lovingly and humbly to God with a cry to be forgiven for our sins – the Spirit comes down upon it and transforms it, as we eat. So we eat and drink together in the bonds of a Love which is infinitely more than any personal affection or attraction we are capable of experiencing for ourselves. 'The peace of God which passeth all understanding be amongst you' – these words uttered at the climax of the Mass, express the truth that we, of ourselves, cannot even understand that peace; still less bring it about. It comes down upon us from above.

There is no 'magic' involved in the words of consecration which constitute the heart of the Eucharistic Sacrifice. The sacrament of Holy Order (or priesting) confers an authorisation, not some mysterious power to turn something into something else. This authorisation is, in certain circumstances, extended: in the final analysis every man and every woman is a priest. So any layman or laywoman, alone on a desert island, may consecrate a palm leaf or a blade of grass, and it will be to him (or her) the Blessed Sacrament of the Body and Blood, exactly as in the Mass. A similar flexibility is illustrated in the moving story of an old priest in a Nazi concentration camp, who was observed to be murmuring the words of consecration over a dirty mug of foul-tasting coffee, which he then drank with profound reverence. A group of fellow prisoners, also Catholics, were shocked; but it was they, not the old priest, who were ignorant: what he did, besides being infinitely touching, was impeccably correct. Behind the words of consecration is the truth that Christ is All-Thing and All-Thing is Christ.

Those words are to be found in the Latin Missal. They are the most sacred words in the language of Christendom; and they should never be pronounced except within the context of the Mass. Ideally, they should never even be written down (they are not hard to remember, after all). Because of their intrinsic holiness, they were the last words to be translated out of the Latin (the language of the Roman Catholic Church) when the Canon of the Mass was vernacularised after Vatican II. Properly, they should be spoken in Latin and almost inaudibly, as the priest bends over the offerings of bread and wine, taking first the Host and then the Chalice in his hands. Next in sacredness are the words of administration. The Anglican Prayer Book version (as always, the best available in English) is as follows:

'The Body of our Lord Jesus Christ which was given for thee, preserve thy body and soul into everlasting life. Take and eat this in remembrance that Christ died for thee, and feed on him in thy heart by faith with thanksgiving.'

As the Chalice is proffered, the word 'drink' is substituted for 'take and eat'; and for 'Body', the word 'Blood'. Until recently the laity of the Church of Rome did not receive the Chalice. The reason for this omission, which has lately been the cause of so vast an amount of discussion and protest, was absurdly simple. It was purely hygienic. Those who understood even a little the meaning of the Blessed Sacrament, understood that it could not make the slightest difference.

The mystery of eating and being eaten is central to virtually every known religion. It is a stage in the process of deification. That which I eat I become. I eat Christ in order that I may be eaten by God. St Augustine of Hippo in the fifth century expressed the matter plainly in words which are nothing if not homely and concrete:

'You did not exist and you were created. You were carried to the Lord's threshing floor. When you were set aside as catechumens you were stored in his barn. You began to be ground with fasting and exorcism. After that you came to water, were moistened and made one. You were cooked then, when the ardour of the Holy Spirit came near, and now have been made the Lord's bread.'

## Chapter Eighteen

# *Time as Sacrament*

The Christian Mystery is the Mystery of Time as Sacrament.

Each one of the six 'extra' sacraments may be 'separated out' of the central Sacrament of the Eucharist. Marking the six stages of Man's life, Baptism, Confirmation, Order, Matrimony, Penance and Extreme Unction may be thought of as the sacraments of a cycle of time, which is brought to its fulfilment in the Eucharistic rite.

The 'six ages' of Man are symbolised in the 'type and antitype' windows of the Middle Ages, by the six waterpots which had to be filled before the miracle of the changing of the water into wine could be accomplished. In an early thirteenth-century window in Canterbury Cathedral, for instance, a picture of the Marriage at Cana is flanked on either side by smaller pictures in which the 'six ages' are depicted, respectively, as six prophets, and as a group consisting of an infant, a schoolboy, a youth, a man in the prime of life, an older man, and a very old man on the verge of death. The miracle at Cana represents the Eucharist. It is a parable of the transformation of earthly into heavenly things, of the life of man into the Life of Christ. The waterpots are 'times'. They are filled up with water, the purificatory element. The life of a man, purified by repentance, is transformed into the New Life in Christ, as the water is changed into wine, and the wine of the Eucharist into Blood. That this miracle should have been performed at a marriage has an obvious significance. The wedding is traditionally supposed to have been between the Magdalen and St John. It is a foretaste of the coming cycle, a similitude of the Marriage in Heaven which fulfils the 'times' When the Mother of Jesus whispers to Him that they have no wine, He turns and says to her with apparent harshness:

## Time as Sacrament

'Woman, what have I to do with thee? Mine *hour* is not yet come.'

This saying recalls the 'harsh' words to the Magdalen in the garden; but the meaning is subtly different. God and man are still separated by *time*. But then He commands that the six waterpots should be filled. The water is passed round and is found to be wine. The marriage is consummated. The times are fulfilled. The Baptism of water 'unto repentance' has become the Baptism of Fire and of Blood.

The sacrament of Baptism corresponds to the beginning of man's life. It has to do with birth. Taken together with Confirmation, it represents the New Birth of which the Lord spoke to Nicodemus: 'Except a man be born of water and the Spirit he cannot enter the Kingdom of God.' Water is a symbol of the pure Virgin as She awaits her fructification by the Holy Spirit. Purified by the waters of repentance, man becomes, for a moment at least, as the Virgin herself. The Spirit descends upon him in that moment; and so in the early Church Baptism and Confirmation were administered together in one rite. In a sense all the sacraments are one. They were separated – like the colours in a prism – for the purpose of sanctifying, one by one, the successive stages of a life in time.

The ancient baptismal ceremonies were of a solemnity which is hard to imagine in an age when few people in their innermost hearts believe in the efficacy of the sacraments. The wealth of symbolism, the beauty and variety of the litanies, hymns and prayers, the sheer length of the rituals performed, marked the moment of transition from 'this world' into the Kingdom of God. The neophyte stood on the 'point of intersection of the timeless with time'. Eternity rushed through him and marked him with the sign of the Cross. This was the Baptism not only of John, but of the One of Whom John said that 'he shall baptise thee with the Holy Ghost and with fire'. It was not at first expected that the baptised person would relapse from the state of sanctification bestowed upon him by the sacrament. He was given his true Name. He was en-Christed. The Church in its beginnings was conceived of by its members as the Community of Saints. Those members looked neither behind nor before (this is the to us inconceivable attitude of mind which has led to the idea that they expected the Second Coming in their own lifetimes) but lived wholly in the present.

## The Christian Mystery

'O truly sacred mysteries!' wrote Clement of Alexandria, who was head of the catechetical school in that city towards the end of the second century AD. 'O pure light! In the blaze of the torches I have a vision of heaven and of God. I become holy by initiation. The Lord reveals the mysteries; He marks the worshipper with His seal, gives light to guide his way, and commends him when he has believed, to the Father's care, where he is guarded for ages to come.'

The symbolism of light was at least as important as that of water in the early baptismal rites; like the holy oils, which were also applied at this time, it represented the Fire of the Holy Spirit. Neophytes (called catechumens) were baptised and anointed at the great ceremony on Easter Eve, when the Paschal candle was lit, and light burst suddenly out of darkness in token of the cataclysmic moment of Resurrection when the body of the Lord dematerialised itself and was remade in a new and spiritualised form as a Body of Heavenly Light. The neophytes, in their white robes, with their new names, held lighted candles in their hands.

In earlier times the neophyte was led into the water and immersed in it. Later, a spoonful was poured over the head only, but the rule remains to this day that it must be *pure* water and it must *flow*. In the ancient prayers of the Church there are many references to a descent into the purifying waters as being the equivalent of burial with Christ. The anointing with chrism symbolised the resurrection and the 'baptism of the Spirit'. Chrism is an unguent made from pure olive oil and corresponds to the element of fire. St Augustine says that 'a man who would enter Paradise must go through fire and water'. The division into two ceremonies, separated in time, of the 'two baptisms' (by water and by oil or fire) has resulted in a great deal of confusion. The baptismal ceremony proper retains its character as the full Christ-baptism, so that in fact it retains within itself the significance of both sacraments; while Confirmation (sometimes misleadingly described as 'the receiving of the Holy Spirit') is a renewal ceremony marking the traditional age for the rites of initiation into adolescence.

The baptism of Jesus in the Jordan is generally regarded as the prototype of the baptismal sacrament. Another scene which recalls the first or 'watery' aspect of the ceremony is that which

## Time as Sacrament

takes place in the Upper Room when Jesus washes the disciples' feet. The timing of this action immediately before the Last Supper parallels the ablution with water *before* the anointing with oil, and the celebration of the baptismal sacrament as a whole *before* the Eucharistic feast. The idea of a *preparation* is present in each case. The dialogue between Jesus and Peter (who invariably represents the Church) is a clue to the significance of what is being done. As the Lord stoops to wash his feet, Peter exclaims: 'Thou shalt never wash my feet!' and the Lord replies: 'If I wash thee not, thou hast no part in Me.' The response of the apostle has been taken as an example of his characteristic 'impulsiveness'. But the so-called 'impulsiveness' of Peter is one of the most finely calculated devices in the New Testament. Invariably a meaning is concealed in it. 'Lord, not my feet only, but also my hands and my head!' This is the request of the Church for immersion in the waters of repentance. But Jesus reassures the 'impulsive' disciple: 'He that is washed, needeth not save to wash his feet . . .'. The meaning here seems to be that the disciples are *already* 'washed'; but their contact with 'this world' (the earth beneath their feet) continuously re-dirties them, and so the washing must be continually renewed. An almost infinite number of shades of meaning are contained within every major episode described in the New Testament. Here there is a connection with Penance, not where the latter is used as *Viaticum* at the end of life, but in its everyday usage as a 'means of grace' for the constantly sinning and re-turning penitent.

The sacrament of Holy Order, or priesting, belongs to man's coming of age, in the sense that it is the formal recognition of his divinely bestowed vocation in relation to the world. Man is the go-between who bears the Divine Life down into the lowest depths of the created world, and raises up the lower realms to be deified in Christ. The mineral, vegetable and animal worlds are all of them present in the body of a man, as are the four elements. This is the meaning of his vocation as a priest. He consecrates the elements; and in his hands they become the Sacred Body and the Sacred Blood. This is the vocation of every man, not only of those men who are set apart and ordained. Ordination is the sacramental bestowal *upon man* of a commission from above. The word 'Order' here has the same meaning as in Simone

Weil's 'the Order of the World'. It refers to the order or pattern of creation which man – and man alone of all created beings – has been appointed to establish, regulate and sustain. This order or pattern is the holding of things together in a state of co-herence. Man is God's agent. In so far as he is faithful to his vocation as a priest, all things owe him obedience.

In a sense there is only one Priest. The sacrament of Order is based upon the idea of a *delegated* priesthood. In the Roman Catholic Church the authority flows from Christ through St Peter to the Pope, and downwards through the bishops, in a system of concentric circles spreading out. The symbolism here is valid regardless of whether or not one accepts the claims of Peter as a matter of historical fact. (There is no doubt that Peter, in the esoteric system which underlies the Gospels, represents the Church.) So the sacrament of Order, which refers in its deeper meaning to the priesting of *man*, refers also to the ordering or delegating of authority with the object of preserving *orderliness* in the administration of the Church. It would not be consistent with *orderliness* for every man and woman to be empowered to consecrate the elements and administer the sacraments.

Ultimately, however, the power is conferred upon us all. The Church has recognised this by its ruling that, in certain circumstances, any man or woman may consecrate 'a blade of grass'. Baptism and absolution are frequently administered by a lay person in the absence of an ordained priest. In the sacrament of matrimony, the priests are regarded as being the man and the woman in the sexual act. In the ceremony of ordination the candidate is solemnly anointed *on his hands*. The immediate significance of this has to do with the power to consecrate the Eucharistic elements; but it has a further meaning, which is that the hands of man are the members whereby he redeems the created world and restores it to God in Christ. The dignity of manual labour is exalted in this sacrament. The 'curse of Adam', whereby he was condemned to 'eat bread in the sweat of thy face', is *turned round* in it, to become the greatest honour possible to bestow upon a creature of this earth.

Holy Matrimony is the sacrament corresponding to the prime of life. The Marriage at Cana is its obvious anti-type in the New Testament; this, however, is no more than a parable of deeper

## Time as Sacrament

mysteries. Because the whole subject of human sexuality is so inextricably intertwined with the innermost esotericism of the Myth, and because the sexual act performed within marriage has a status equal to that of the Eucharistic rite, we shall devote a separate chapter to this sacrament.

Penance (generally referred to as 'Confession') is a *preparation* for the hour of death. In India, when a householder has passed the prime of life, he abandons his family and friends, divests himself of his possessions, and adopts the existence of a wandering mendicant. The sacrament of Penance has to do with a similar idea. Used regularly as a preparation for Communion (in itself a passage through death in so far as it is properly accepted and understood), it is *essentially* the rite of repentance and re-turning at the approach of life's end. The penitent confesses his (or her) sins, receives absolution and is given a penance. The entire action consists of a stripping of oneself before God. The Church has prescribed this sacrament as being formally necessary on three occasions: as an annual preparation for the Easter Communion; as the rite of re-turn in a case of 'mortal sin'; and as an integral part of *Viaticum* or the Last Rites, when it is administered regardless of whether or not the penitent is physically capable of confessing his sins to a priest. The injunction relating to 'mortal' sin is necessary and inevitable; but can easily mislead.

'Mortal' sin, in this world, is a theoretical possibility (like Hell) but in practice it is virtually impossible to commit. As a wise priest once remarked: 'Mortal sin can only be committed by the saints; and the saints do not commit mortal sin.' He meant that since, by the Church's definition, mortal sin can only be committed in full knowledge of what one is doing and with the full consent of the will to do it, the vast majority of human beings are exempt from it in this life, being totally incapable of such undimmed vision, and such ingathered simplicity in their acts. As Gurdjieff never tired of repeating: 'Man cannot *do*' – ordinary men at least; man who is half-asleep. 'Doing' in this sense is reserved for very few. Properly understood, the sacrament of Penance refers to Adam's sin. In this sin every man participates, as also in the penance it incurs, which is death itself; yet in Christ he is released from both.

By loving and devout Catholics, this sacrament of the hour of death is regularly used as a 'means of grace'. As such it is a deliberate placing of oneself at the metaphysical centre, the 'place of the heart' where the power of the Holy Spirit is invoked. The penitent is told to 'make a good act of contrition' while confessing his sins. An 'act' in the terminology of the Church, is an inward turning of the will. The 'matter' of the sacrament is sin. What is actually being confessed is the participation of the penitent in Adam's sin. His everyday or 'venial' sins are linked with this; even while they themselves are no more than 'stains on the soles of the feet'.

The last of the 'extra' sacraments is the final sealing of the body and the soul as the moment of their separation becomes imminent. This is known as Extreme Unction because it is administered (together with Penance and Communion, the three together being known as the Last Rites) in the extremity of death. The dying person is anointed on the eyes, ears, nostrils, mouth, hands and feet. As he performs the rite, the priest says (in Latin):

'By this holy anointing and his merciful loving kindness may the Lord forgive you all the sins you have committed through the sense of sight . . . hearing . . . smell . . . speech and the sense of taste . . . touch . . . power of motion. Amen.'

These prayers emphasise the cleansing and forgiving aspect of the sacrament. But it has another, and perhaps even deeper meaning in the *sealing*, through the body, of the soul. In many of the ancient rites of baptismal anointing the oil or chrism is described as a 'seal' throughout. An Armenian ritual prayer evokes this theme:

'A fragrant oil poured out in the name of Christ, the *seal* of heavenly gifts . . . This *seal* which is in the name of Christ, may it enlighten thine eyes that thou mayest not ever sleep in death . . . May this *seal* of Christ be to thee for a sweet smell from life to life . . . May the divine *seal* guide thy steps aright into life immortal.'

One is reminded of how Jesus Himself retired into the shadows of the oil-bearing tree to prepare for His own death, and of how His body was anointed before it was laid in the tomb.

The sacrament of Extreme Unction is intended to be administered when the recipient is about to die. It is *not* essentially a sacrament for the healing of sickness or for the

## Time as Sacrament

blessing of a sick person, and any attempt to reduce it to this status is sheer sentimentality and evasiveness. It is a rite of passage, an initiation ceremony in the presence of death. Afterwards, certain prayers are prescribed for comforting and speeding the departing soul. Time was when people were more frightened of dying without this sacrament than of death itself. They understood that the physical healing of the sick is not comparably so important as preparing the dying and showing them *how to die*. Jesus and His disciples practised healing as a matter of course. They laid their hands upon the sick; and many Christians, finding themselves possessed of this spiritual gift, have in charity done the same. But physical health is unimportant compared with that skill in the 'craft of dying' which is taught, for instance, in the beautiful medieval treatise of that name, in which are to be found these words:

'Against his will he dieth that hath not learned to die. Learn to die and thou shalt learn to live, for there shall none learn to live that hath not learned to die.'

Not many years ago a nun died at the Cistercian nunnery of La Trappe in Dorset. The ceremonies accompanying her death had remained unchanged since AD 1098. (Perhaps they are still unchanged today: anything is possible in that tiny centre of contemplative prayer and silence.) When the Sister was known to be dying, a wooden rattle was sounded, to be heard all over the Convent. Every Sister left what she was doing and hurried instantly to the Infirmary, where the whole Community gathered beside the bed. The nun had already made her confession in private. During the administration of *Viaticum* and the Last Anointing the Community knelt, making the responses at appropriate moments. Afterwards they continued to kneel, while prayers and litanies for the dying were recited, patiently, unhurriedly, as a matter of course, for so long as the soul lingered. When at last she was gone, a great Paschal candle was lit at the foot of the bed; and the body was left for one hour alone and in absolute silence. 'So that the soul may go gently' is the explanation given for this practice. That done, the infirmarian washed the body and clothed it in the habit. A nun gathered fresh flowers in the garden. Another wove them into a circlet representing the heavenly crown, which was placed upon the Sister's head. Then six nuns carried the body to the chapel and

## The Christian Mystery

laid it, facing the altar, on a bier. The Paschal candle was placed at the head of this bier. For the rest of the day and the next night the body was watched by two nuns, reciting psalms ('Yea, though I walk through the valley of the shadow of death I will fear no evil'). The following day in the afternoon the Community sang the Requiem Mass, after which they carried their Sister to her grave, still singing, always the sublime music of Gregorian chant. In their little walled cemetery they laid her uncoffined body on the bare earth and stood on either side of it in two rows. The priest blessed the grave and hallowed it with incense. Then six Sisters lowered the body on wide bands of linen. Two more dropped soil on it very softly; and while this was being done the whole Community knelt, bowing to the ground and touching it with their knuckles as Cistercians do, chanting three times:

*Domine miserere super peccatrice.*

In a ceremony such as this we may see the meaning of death in Christ.

## Chapter Nineteen

# *Man as Sacrament*

Holy Matrimony is the Sacrament of Man. It digs down to the roots of his being, to the sexual act which is the moment of his coming-to-be, his human ecstasy and his 'little death'. It is the hardest to understand of all the Church's sacraments. As has already been remarked, its status is equal to that of the Eucharist itself. In it, the man and the woman, acting as their own priests, *redeem* the act of sex.

The actual ceremony in the presence of the priest is *not* the sacrament. (The simplest Catholic understands this; although non-Catholics frequently do not.) It is held to be necessary, because it is the solemn affirmation, in the presence of the Community of Christians, that the act will be performed *in Christ*. The act itself is the 'matter' of the sacrament. One reason for the absolute prohibition against infidelity is that *all* the subsequent sexual acts between the couple are regarded as being coinherent, each in each, so that an act undertaken outside this coinherence destroys it at once. So far the meaning is not difficult to grasp. The harshness comes with the teaching that sexual acts *outside* the marriage sacrament are, by definition, sin. This teaching is generally misunderstood. When it is understood, it remains hard; but in another sense.

The Church's affirmation of sex as sacrament is based upon a metaphysical truth which is not limited by *rules*. The *rules* which have been devised for the *protection* of the sacrament are not in themselves intended to be regarded as absolute. These rules include the provision of a ceremony performed in the presence of a priest. But the Church has never explicitly defined what it is that transforms what would otherwise be sin into sacrament, except by declaring that sexuality becomes sacrament *in Christ*.

The ceremony and the 'ring' are in a sense irrelevant. It is enormously significant that the Church has always asserted its power to annul any marriage if it chooses to do so. Annulments were at one time quite openly *bought* – and, without excusing this nefarious practice, we can learn from it. The insistence was not upon some 'magical' efficacy inherent in the ceremony itself, but simply upon obedience to a necessary rule. The area of sexual activity is regarded as being so fraught with the danger of falling into sin that the Church has assumed the right to enclose it very strictly and precisely within bounds. What is really being said is that the act of generation must *either* be 'in Christ' or 'in death'.

If the Church's teachings about sex appear relentless, their uncompromising nature has nothing whatsoever to do with notions of 'dirtiness' in connection with the sexual act. Many Christians have been guilty of prurience: the Church, never. The Church has a relentless view not only of sex but of man himself, as being sick unto death except *in so far as* he returns *in all things* and *by all ways* to God in Christ. In a catastrophically falling world to generate another human being would be a sin. And our world *is* catastrophically falling *in so far as* it is not 'in Christ', in Whom it becomes the Eucharistic Sacrament. Here in 'this world', we are *poised* between the world of the Fall and the redeemed world of the Kingdom of God. In one sense the Act of Creation is in itself the Fall. The act of sex (which on the human plane corresponds to that Eternal Act) coinheres on the one hand with the Marriage in Heaven; on the other with the Death of the Cross. The orgasm and the cry of dereliction are eternally one, as the Son of God falls into the Void, and draws up, *ex nihilo*, out of nothing, the Created One of God, His Love and His Cross. These things are mysteries too deep for the Church to have attempted, exoterically, to explain. The Church cannot justify its own relentlessness in terms which can be generally understood. The act of generation is the very process of the splitting up into the many of the One; but when the Church, for this reason, defines it as the perpetuation of the Fall, this is interpreted as meaning that sex is in some way 'unclean' in itself. Whosoever performs the sexual act *outside* the coinherence of the Mystical Church, of necessity participates in the Crucifixion of the Son of God: this is the relentless logic of the Myth; but, when it is put into words, those words are misinterpreted at once.

## Man as Sacrament

The sacrament of Holy Matrimony is by definition the performance of the sexual act *within* the Coinherence, *within* the Mystical Church, as the very sign and symbol of the deification of the human soul *on the other side of death*. Because it must be a passage through death it involves on the human side a total self-sacrifice in love. The Anglican Prayer Book defines it as 'signifying the mystical union that is betwixt Christ and his Church'. Within that meaning is another: the union of spirit and soul in the depths of the heart. Throughout the entire field of mythology, including the fairy-tales of princes and princesses who come together after various adventures and ordeals (including, frequently, a symbolic death and resurrection as in the stories of the Sleeping Beauty and Snow White), we shall find every time that the marriage between the human being and the god, or between the princess and the King or Prince, represents the *drawing up* into the realm of spirit of the human soul, together with the animal nature – which generally appears in these stories as an actual animal or a servant. In the ubiquitous tale of the deserted princess whose role as the bride is usurped by her maid, the theme is that of the spiritual principle (the prince) which reclaims the soul from the lower nature (the servant) which has dragged it down and cast it out. (One of the finest of these stories is 'The Goose Girl', where the 'good' and faithful aspect of the animal nature is represented by Falada, the beheaded horse.) In the 'Snow White' type of story, on the other hand, the princess is served by good, hard-working creatures, typically 'dwarfs', who show how the function of the physical body is to guard the soul until the coming of her Lord. In all these traditional tales the idea recurs and recurs that marriage is the ultimate good providing the pairing is correct and the right princess marries the right prince. They are all a reflection, in their own way, of the Christian Myth.

But if human sexuality *can be* a participation in glory, it *tends to be* a participation in the primal sin, the Luciferian experience of *ecstasy for its own sake*. It is this primal sin which brings about the Crucifixion of the Christ. Indeed the Crucifixion *is* this sin. The Church, one suspects, would have actually put a ban upon sex, prohibiting it altogether as too sacred and too dangerous to be touched, had this been a practicable measure; and, since it was not, the alternative was to affirm it as a sacrament, and then hedge it about with prohibitions and taboos. Theoretically, this explicit affirmation need not have been made. Theoretically, the Marriage Sacrament could have remained implicit – as it were secreted – in the Eucharistic rite; while the Church became a Community of monks and nuns awaiting the Second Coming of the Christ. This alone would have been considered safe; and in the first few years of the Church's existence it doubtless seemed possible as well. In those years it is probable that virginity was regarded as the norm, and existing spouses were counselled to practise abstinence in so far as they reasonably could. The Church was 'the Community of Saints'. The sole purpose of marriage was to generate souls for the Kingdom of God; and that purpose was admitted only after it became clear that the Coming of the Kingdom was not necessarily imminent. The 'world' for those Christians stood over against them. The idea of the mass-conversion of society itself was not in their minds. When this came about the Church suffered a shock from which it has never recovered itself. The rules that were laid down for a community of saints stayed exactly as they were – and were found to be, generally speaking, impossible to keep. But the sacrament of Penance was a bottomless well of inestimable comfort: sins of disobedience poured into it in a never-ending flood and vanished from sight. The Monastic Orders were formed in a not wholly logical attempt to distil out of a compromised and compromising Christian world what was originally thought of as the Christian way of life.

It is hardly surprising perhaps that many, if not all, the traditions have contained within themselves closely secluded circles devoted to the practice of rituals based upon the Mystery of sex. The iconography of Tantric Hinduism and Buddhism arose out of such cults and the type of mysticism they represent. Generally speaking, they involve a relationship between a man and a woman leading up to but not including the climax of the sexual act. In the more extreme (and hard to imagine) tantric practices the climax is reached and the male sperm is withdrawn at the same moment. Beneath all this is the concept of the drawing down of spiritual power from above. Legitimate spiritual power – or not? The dangers are apparent and extreme. The church has consistently frowned upon such practices, which were none the less common in Christian gnostic communities in

## Man as Sacrament

the first few centuries after Christ. In its beginnings the most wholly esoteric of all the traditions, the Christian religion became for that very reason the most formalised and apparently exoteric. The esotericism was buried beneath formulas, the dangers were evaded by the laws. The emphasis fell upon obedience. But still in the high Middle Ages the troubadours sang of a love which was chaste and yet passionately intense, enabling the lover to soar beyond it into regions of mystical experience. Dante is, of course, the greatest of all the exponents of this love. The death of his Beatrice resembles, in his poetry, the Dark Night of the Soul of St John of the Cross. Emerging from that Night, he finds in her memory an object of contemplation which, deliberately cultivated and used, is sufficiently transparent to merge into the image of the Virgin Herself. At the climax of the *Paradiso*, it blends into the Heavenly Vision of the Coinherence of All-Thing in God. His Beatrice is lost in the centre of the Mystical Rose.

This medieval cult has proved to be impossible to eradicate. Strangely but inevitably, the Church has consistently endeavoured to eradicate it. Dante's love, on account of its chastity, was conceded to be legitimate. But the cult of such loves was ultimately incompatible with the institution of marriage as sacrament. Its dangers were numerous and apparent, the most obvious being that the majority of such passions were unlikely to remain chaste very long. The Church was not greatly concerned with the raptures of mystical experience however arrived at; its concern was the re-turning of the world and the salvation of souls. It preferred to lay stress upon the Religious Orders as providing an opportunity for contemplative prayer and an initiatory path to the Vision of God. And even here, when the vision became ecstatic, there was wariness and mistrust. The raptures of the mystics and the sexual symbolism they used in describing those raptures – which is more than mere 'symbolism', as the experiences themselves arise from the coinherence of the soul in the Divine Nuptials at the Heart of the World – were almost as unnerving to ecclesiastical officialdom as the love songs of the troubadours (which were far less unashamedly sensual and explicit). If all this could have been put down it would have been, no doubt – just as the too exposed esotericism of Gnosticism was put down, thereby being driven into forms

## The Christian Mystery

that became increasingly wayward and eccentric. And indeed it would seem that, in our own times, by methods more effectual even than the Inquisition itself, official Christianity has succeeded at last in eradicating from the Church the entire esoteric and mystical content of the Myth.

Meanwhile, as we contemplate the sacrament of Marriage, so prosaic, so practical, so infinite in its outreach to divine realities on the other side of death, we shall find its innermost significance in those mystical writings which are wholly concerned with the things of God presented under the similitude of sexual love. St John of the Cross was directly influenced by the Song of Songs, an affinity which is clear in one of his most beautiful and extraordinary poems, entitled 'Song of the Soul in rapture at having arrived by the road of negation at the state of union with God':

> Upon a gloomy night,
> With all my cares to loving ardours flushed,
> (O venture of delight!)
> With nobody in sight
> I went abroad when all my house was hushed.
>
> In safety, in disguise,
> In darkness up the secret stair I crept,
> (O happy enterprise)
> Concealed from other eyes
> When all my house at length in silence slept.
>
> Upon that lucky night
> In secrecy, inscrutable to sight,
> I went without discerning
> And with no other light
> Except for that which in my heart was burning.
>
> It lit and led me through
> More certain than the light of noonday clear
> To where One waited near
> Whose presence well I knew,
> There where no other presence might appear.

## Man as Sacrament

O night that was my guide!
O darkness dearer than the morning's pride,
O night that joined the lover
To the beloved bride
Transfiguring them each into the other.

Within my flowering breast
Which only for himself entire I save
He sank into his rest
And all my gifts I gave
Lulled by the airs with which the cedars wave.

Over the ramparts fanned
While the fresh wind was fluttering his tresses,
With his serenest hand
My neck he wounded, and
Suspended every sense with its caresses.

Lost to myself I stayed
My face upon my lover having laid
From all endeavour ceasing:
And all my cares releasing
Threw them amongst the lilies there to fade.

That is the Mystical Marriage of which all marriages in Christ are the similitude and the sacrament. From that ecstatic union flows the grace which, in aridity and tiredness, baths the baby, shops in the supermarket, forgives the adulteries and pays the rent.

## Chapter Twenty

# *God as Sacrament*

The greatest of all sacraments is the Blessed Sacrament Itself, the Sacred Host. This is, by a convention, the metaphysical centre in which all things coinhere, and from which the Love of God streams forth. It is the simplest object that could possibly have been devised for the purpose: a paper-thin, round, white wafer-biscuit, indistinguishable from any other under chemical analysis. There are a multitude of Hosts, yet there is but One, since all are contained in each one. In the Host is contained the whole world enclosed within the Body of Christ. The Host is not the Body as distinct from the Blood (which is why it makes no difference to Catholics whether they receive Communion 'in one kind' or in both) nor is It Christ as distinct from the world. It is All-Thing and All-Men and the Ultimate Blessedness of God enclosed within a very little space, but not limited by that space, reaching out from it to englobe the universe itself. All space and all times are *here* and *present* in this tiny thing. This is so, not on account of some 'magical' transformation wrought by a priest, but by an Act of Faith. The Church, in its adoration of the Blessed Sacrament affirms its faith in *that which is*.

The is-ness of the world and of everything in it *is* in Christ. All that is 'outside' Christ *is not*; although, having said this, we must instantly correct it by saying that Christ, the Divine Son, englobes the 'is-not' by drawing it into His splayed out Body on the Cross. In Christ the 'is-not' is overcome. But for us, in 'this world', its power continues *temporarily* to be felt. The quality of *unrealness* in 'this world' belongs to the no-thing to which (because it is 'ourselves') we are still attracted in opposition to the Love of God. But the Church has declared that in *one thing* at least the Godhead shall be affirmed by us as being wholly

## God as Sacrament

Present. That one thing is the Sacred Host. The Sacred Host, is what It is, not by its own nature as a creature but by virtue of Its Divine Essence; since every created thing down to the tiniest atom beneath the microscope *is* only God. It is what It is by the faith of the Church that in this One Thing the faithful are being permitted to turn away wholly from the unrealities of this dreamlike world, and contemplate the Only Truth. For the world is God or it is not-God *as we choose that it shall be*. If we could but *choose that it should be so*, our entire world would become the Blessed Sacrament. But we 'cannot', by definition, in this world, so choose. The most we can do is to set aside a tiny space and consent together to That. Within that tiny space we may then find all the worlds; from It in all the directions the worlds blossom outwards to englobe the Void. It is the Perfect Flower, the Rose blooming outwards from the Cross. All this It *is* of Itself. We could choose any thing in the world and it would be the same. But we *can* only choose one thing. If we could worship *all things as they are* in God we should not be still in 'this world', we should find ourselves in Heaven Itself. And we do not so find ourselves. Not yet. The time is being worked out.

The Sufi mystic Ansari, although he was not of course writing specifically of the Christian sacraments, explains the matter perfectly in a few words:

> What is worship?
> It is reality.

The Blessed Sacrament has been, for centuries now, the central Mystery of the Roman Catholic Church. Devotion to this Mystery has united all Catholics, from the learned theologian to the illiterate peasant. In this devotion all are equal, in that it transcends the highest reaches of the human mind, eludes intellectual analysis, and is potentially capable of bringing together the entire human race in one simple prayer of humility and love. Up till a short time ago (for one has to say in passing that the Roman Catholic Church has temporarily abandoned all the more esoteric and mystical aspects of its faith) the service of Benediction, as this was conducted in any Catholic church in any part of the world, provided a moving illustration of what this devotion meant to Catholics, of every imaginable kind, irrespective of nationality, class, opinion, ability or temperament. Throughout this service of adoration the Blessed Sacrament is exposed in a monstrance. This round glass 'locket' (frequently encircled by golden 'rays' to produce the effect of a sunburst) is placed on a high platform above the altar, where all can fix their eyes upon it. The Sacrament is visible behind the glass. It is (or was, for the custom is dying out) customary for the faithful, instead of genuflecting on one knee as they would normally do in passing the Host enclosed in the tabernacle, to adore the Exposed Sacrament by falling on both knees, touching their foreheads to the ground. The rite of Benediction lasts rather less than half an hour. It is composed mainly of ancient Latin hymns of adoration set to the Gregorian chant, and culminates in the blessing of the people by the upraised Sacrament. It ends with the heart's cry of the Church:

*Adoremus in aeternum Sanctissimum Sacramentum*

Mother Teresa of Calcutta has said publicly several times that without the strength she receives from the Blessed Sacrament she could not do her work. 'If we can see Jesus', she says, 'in the appearance of bread, we can see Him in the bodies of the poor.' This is a wonderful definition of the meaning of the Blessed Sacrament, expressing the idea that It must be continuously extending Itself and gathering up the world into a single point. 'I saw God in a point,' says Julian of Norwich, 'by which I saw that He is in all things.' If Mother Teresa were to be deprived of the sacraments of the Church, she would not thereby feel deprived of the Blessed Sacrament or of Christ: these – or, more accurately, This – would be there for her still in the festering, vomit-smeared bodies she brings in from the street. She is one of those rare persons who have earned the right to define for us the meaning of love. She says: 'To belong fully to God we have to give up everything. Only then can we truly love.'

Love is not a 'feeling'; it is not necessarily even a doing-good. It is not 'personal' in the sense in which that word is most commonly used. If we confuse it with our personal feelings towards our friends, we run the risk of making sentimental and basically insincere approaches to the people we meet. Nothing is more depressing than the kind of would-be 'Christian' bonhomie

## God as Sacrament

which treats everyone indiscriminately as a personal friend. On the other hand, love is not impersonal in the sense of being unparticularised and cold. The distinction between true love and the extraordinary variety of emotional reactions which pass under that name, is that true love is *for all things particularised in one*. This strange state which, paradoxical as it is, is clearly recognisable in experience, only becomes possible for us in Christ. In it we are being caught up into the Love within the Trinity whereby God loves Himself. We love the other person for being God's. We love the tiny creature – bird, insect, mouse, no matter what – which lies in the palm of the hand, because this one and none other is, for us, at this moment the Beloved of God. Such an experience of love is an extension of our adoration of the Blessed Sacrament. *This* person, *this* creature, *this* tiny scrap of bread which derives its reality solely from Him, this and none other is GOD: not that all others are excluded from this; but that all others are included in this One. 'He shewed me', writes Julian of Norwich, 'a little thing the size of a hazel nut which seemed to lie in the palm of my hand and it was as round as any ball. I looked upon it with the eye of my understanding and thought: What may this be? I was answered in a general way thus: It is all that is made. In this little thing I saw three properties: that God made it; that God loveth it; that God keepeth it.'

In the Mystery of the Blessed Sacrament the Church goes further still and affirms:

'God deifies it.'

The Christian Mystery is the Mystery of God as Sacrament.

For Product Safety Concerns and Information please contact our EU
representative  GPSR@taylorandfrancis.com
Taylor & Francis Verlag GmbH, Kaufingerstraße 24, 80331 München, Germany

www.ingramcontent.com/pod-product-compliance
Lightning Source LLC
Chambersburg PA
CBHW070621300426
44113CB00010B/1606